# YES

**A Visual Biography
I: 1968 – 1981**

**Martin Popoff**

# YES

## A Visual Biography
## I: 1968 – 1981

**Martin Popoff**

**WP**
**WYMER**
PUBLISHING
Bedford, England

First published in Great Britain in 2021
by Wymer Publishing
www.wymerpublishing.co.uk
Tel: 01234 326691
Wymer Publishing is a trading name of Wymer (UK) Ltd

Revised edition, 2022
Copyright © Martin Popoff /Wymer Publishing.

ISBN: 978-1-912782-98-7

The Author hereby asserts his rights to be identified
as the author of this work in accordance with sections
77 to 78 of the Copyright, Designs & Patents Act 1988.

All rights reserved. No part of this publication may be
reproduced or transmitted in any form or by any means,
electronic or mechanical, including photocopying, or any
information storage and retrieval system, without written
permission from the publisher.

This publication is sold subject to the condition that it shall not,
by way of trade or otherwise, be lent, re-sold, hired out or
otherwise circulated without the publishers prior consent in any
form of binding or cover other than that in which it is published
and without a similar condition including this condition
being imposed on the subsequent purchaser.

Every effort has been made to trace the copyright holders of the
photographs in this book but some were unreachable. We would
be grateful if the photographers concerned would contact us.

Design by Andy Bishop / 1016 Sarpsborg
Printed by Imago Group.

A catalogue record for this book is available from the British Library.

**Yes: A Visual Biography I: 1968 – 1981**

Martin Popoff

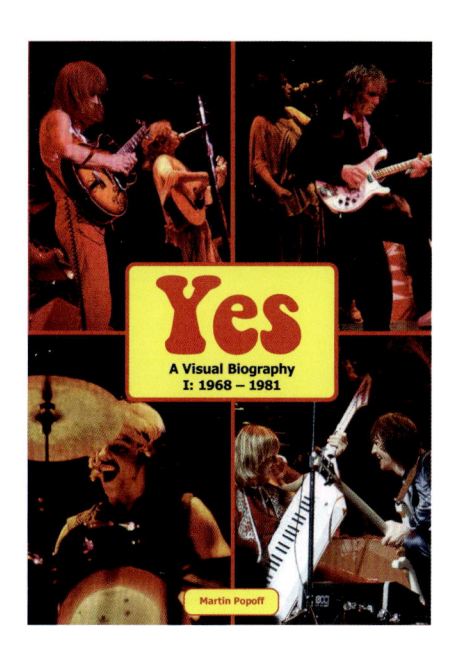

Dedicated to Chris Squire...
...the engine of Yes from the genesis.

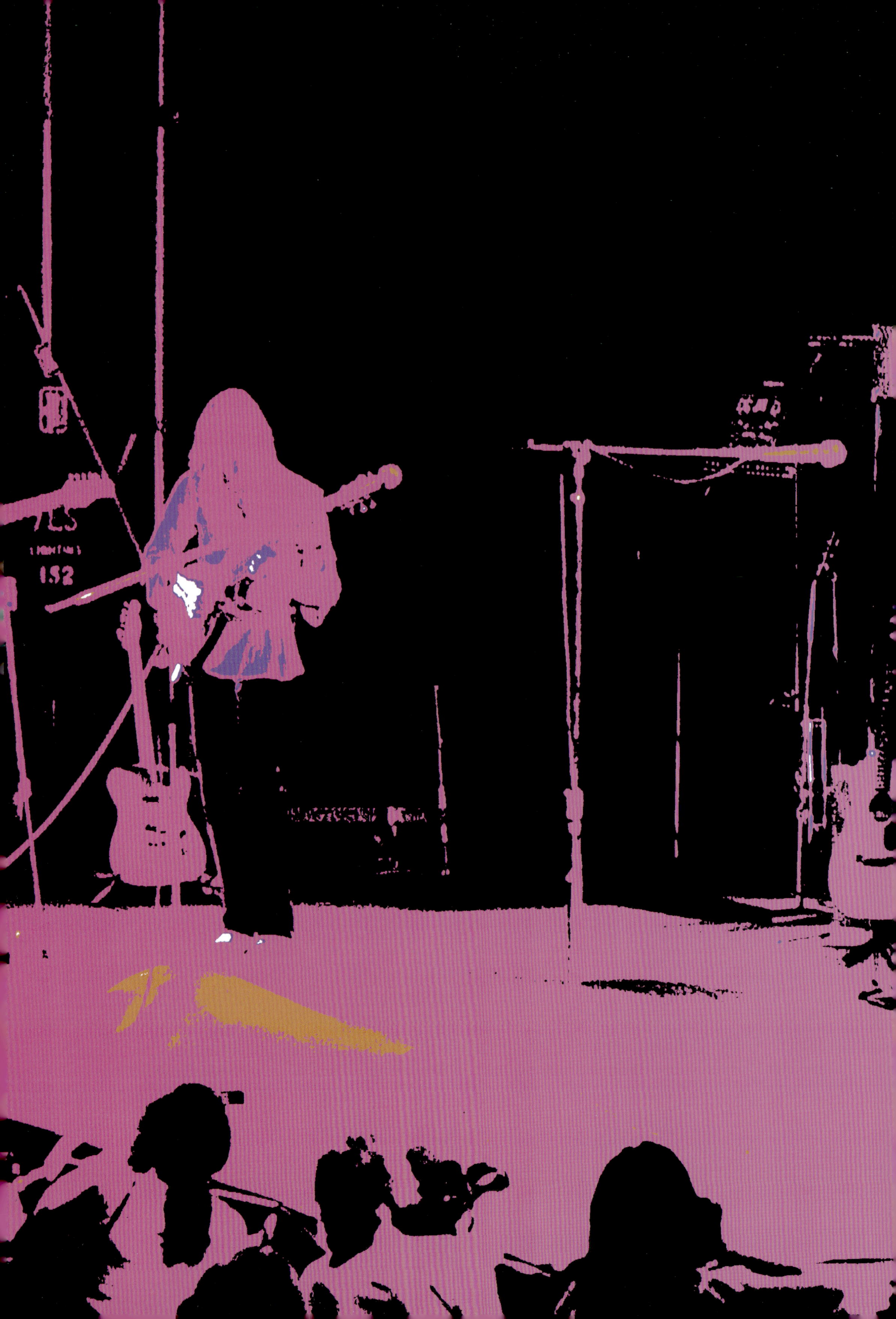

# CONTENTS

| | |
|---|---|
| Introduction | 9 |
| Origins Through 1969: *Yes* | 15 |
| 1970: *Time and a Word* | 35 |
| 1971: *The Yes Album* and *Fragile* | 45 |
| 1972: *Close to the Edge* | 61 |
| 1973: *Tales from Topographic Oceans* | 79 |
| 1974 to 1976: *Relayer* | 105 |
| 1977: *Going for the One* | 139 |
| 1978 to 1979: *Tormato* | 161 |
| 1980 to 1981: *Drama* | 191 |
| Selected Discography | 217 |
| Interviews by the Author | 219 |
| Additional Citations | 221 |
| Special Thanks | 221 |
| Martin Popoff – A Complete Bibliography | 222 |
| About the Author | 224 |

September 29th, 1978, Tulsa Assembly Center, Tulsa OK.

© Rich Galbraith

# Introduction

Welcome prog-heads and idealistic art rockers one and all to this sumptuous celebration of the greatest progressive rock band of all time, yes, Yes.

As you may know, I've done a few of these picture-stuffed coffee table books with the good people at Wymer Publishing, but I would say this is the richest yet, with respect to the wordplay at play. Now, an explanation is in order. What I've done here is re-purpose the writing I did within a long out-of-print Yes book I wrote called *Time and a Word*, arriving at this place extremely gleeful that those words, framed upon a timeline, are now back in circulation, and furthermore, buttressed by all manner of photography, which is really what these "visual biographies" are all about anyway.

But here's the thing, I've added numerous quotes, done a ton of rewriting and repositioning and even threw in a few more timeline entries. However, the most significant change is that with the current volume, we are examining the band's first ten studio albums only, along with everything that happened in-between—the touring, the solo projects, etc.

To be sure, there are plans for a follow-up volume (or two), but that is a different conversation. For now, the plan is to relive the origins of the band in the late '60s, through to the final studio album of ten, *Drama*, and the tour cycle that great and underrated record generated.

Must say it's been a pleasure writing now a second book on progressive rock pioneers Yes, having been a fan since the late '70s. Indeed, Yes would've been one of the very first bands that wasn't a hard rockin' heavy metal (or punk!) band that I ever patronized and respected and let into my quickly literary-inclined life, high school into university, into more university and then work life.

Gateway into Yes was the fact that I was an aspiring drummer, and upon my white Pearl nine-piece set, I tapped away at the likes of *Going for the One*, *Drama*, and… well, definitely not *Close to the Edge*, *Tales from Topographic Oceans* and *Relayer*, because that would've been too difficult.

So here we are, looking at a book that was a joy to write because it allowed me to go back and play all this great music yet again, from so many different eras, with so many different lineups even within the context of only ten records, and to put remarks from the band, myself and others on that music into some kind of logical order.

Chronological order, that is. I knew from the outset that when I was going to tackle anything on this band, I had to use the timeline with quotes format that I first adopted with my *Deep Purple Royal Family* duo of books, and many times again over the years. What I like about this format applies particularly well when a band has as complex a history as does Yes. Because most pertinently with my *Deep Purple Royal Family* two-book set, the idea also here was to include much of the solo album and side collaboration experiences so that one could see, using tight chronology, when these things happened in relation to Yes albums and tours. Now, point of clarification, I

September 29th, 1978, Tulsa Assembly Center, Tulsa, OK

put limits on how extensive I would address solo careers, first and foremost because Rick Wakeman himself has put out something like a hundred albums. Additionally, however, I didn't include solo works by everybody who was ever a part of Yes, but stuck mainly to chief members of the band.

And then there are grey areas, people like original drummer Bill Bruford, who wasn't around for that long, but did a couple of solo records in the late '70s that are essentially considered part of the progressive rock family, or, in other words, somewhat of interest to many Yes fans. As well, on this solo front, I tried not to offer elucidating quotes for everything, even if it was a record by a major member of the band. Still, I get a kick out of the fact that this might be the only book where any of this triplet-ravaged tributary of the Yes river is discussed to any degree at all. Suffice to say that in general, we more than dip our toe in the roiling solo waters, but we don't submerge fully lest the current... okay, enough.

Also, what I like to do with these timeline things, as I've done here, is that I've included some major milestones from other big prog bands related to Yes, or even just considered part of the progressive rock story, and thus shed some mirrored light on Yes' career and vice versa, vis-à-vis Yes' relationship with the outside world.

A few other points of structure, just in case you noticed these foibles and were scratching your head. If I only knew year of an event, and not month, that entry would go at the start of the entries for that year. Drilling down, October 1976 will be listed before any entry for which we know what day in October something happened. You will also see that I have introductions to each year, and the thinking here is that I'm trying not to infuse too much opinion into the entries, leaving them pretty much informational, and then letting the Yes member or journalist or what have you, say their piece as an explanation of the entry.

But I indeed wanted to say my piece, as that is one of the satisfying parts of doing these books, whether it be this way, or the typical narrative paragraph method, which I've utilized for 15 or 20 of these rock biographies as well. So the introductory sections for each year are the locales at which I get to reflect, shoot off my mouth, give you a glimpse of what I think of the band's material during this time, and, indeed, provide an overview of the salient elements of what happened to the band over period you are about to wander amongst and relive.

Additional to this, I've included a scatter of reviews I'd written for various magazines as well as in advance of a book where I had planned to review all the Yes albums and most of the offshoot solo works. The aim here is as above, to inject a little more analysis of the art on my part, in balance against the scholarly feel of our timeline with oral history approach. But although I've included quite a few of these, I didn't go too crazy, leaving the running dialogue of the band not too, too obscured or interrupted. As well, I scattered 'em around, providing a balance between band and satellite project. I figured it still felt right, given that I've included the odd review from outside journalists, as well as the fact that I've quipped a bit myself directly within entries. When they show up, take 'em in the spirit of a sidebar, a pause to reflect a little more deeply on what matters the most in all this—the recorded works.

So that's about it. To reiterate, again, this is a band that has given me much joy over the years, first from a progressive rock point of view that so many musicians and players enjoy, but also just because of my love of such high-quality and such varied music. The Utopian world Jon resolutely if

# chris squire

1970s Atlantic Records promo photo.

nowhere near methodically created through his growing lyrical canon over the years... it can't be anything but good for the heart to be confronted with such optimism so enigmatically put year after year now for over five decades. As for the expanded catalogue, I've been a fan of many of Jon Anderson's solo albums and love the second Steve Howe album as much as many Yes albums, and actually think that Chris Squire's *Fish Out of Water* ranks up there with the very best handful of actual Yes albums.

As well, it's been rich and rewarding doing this book because it reminded me of how as I've grown older decade by decade, I've interacted with the band at all these different junctures within their career, celebrating and cheering on that second wind that they got with *90125* (hopefully to be addressed in a second volume!), actually seeing the band live for the first time during that tour, and then touching down upon so many of the albums after that, as well as beginning to interview the band regularly through the '90s and 2000s. In tandem with that, of course, I've been able to experience the band many more times live, and it's always a treat to witness the milestone music from the era covered in this book brought to life, in every instance to packed houses, at least every time that I've been there.

So, enough of my blather, without further adieu, come relive with me these times again, using a format that really reminds us to think rigorously about time, and, through the adjunct quote process... a word!

Martin Popoff
martinp@inforamp.net; martinpopoff.com

"Chris Squire was the slow one, always. Chris was very solid in the bass department; he had a very unique sound. Chris was also the one who would think things over carefully; he was never impetuous. He was very slow and methodical—painfully slow in everything. Chris was the same as he had always been in the other bands we were in together. I mean, it would take two hours to get out of bed and another hour to have breakfast and so on—nothing had changed. He and Bill Bruford made a real powerhouse rhythm monster cooking in the boiler room. Chris used to think of his bass as a second lead guitar. At times it meant that he and I would be at the top of the neck, the consequence of which meant all the bottom end of the group would disappear, frustrating the hell out of Bill. This kind of friction would sometimes work to our advantage."
**Peter Banks**

# Origins Through 1969: Yes

© Laurens Van Houten / Frank White Photo Agency

As we begin our tale, timeline, time with a word, what, essentially, do we see from the members of Yes in their formative years?

Well, through fairly unremarkable childhoods, each and all strike an interest in—and a propensity for—music. Quite interesting, theories abound how progressive rock is so intrinsically British, where in America, few bands of this ilk emerged from the late '60s into the '70s. One fairly accepted theory is that Europe is the birthplace, the cradle, of classical music, whereas in America, it is the nation's rich blues-based tradition that informs rock history. Not to slight the rest of Europe, many countries had their prog tradition and a monster band or two, and that just supports the theory that sorta 400 years of classical music is in the blood over there more than anywhere else.

As well, arguably, and depending on region, music programs have always been said to be better in Europe than in America, and more classical-based, more traditional in keeping with every facet of life being more traditional. In any event, here come our heroes, receiving signals from centuries of classical music, the birth of the Beatles (proudly representing a taking-over of this new music, an invasion), and then psychedelia, which, granted, was both homegrown, and imported from San Francisco.

The big story pre-1970, of which Yes plays only a component part, is the establishment of a proto-progressive rock movement, or even the *idea* of a movement, necessarily welling up from the mind-expansion that was psych rock. Following on is the establishment of an album rock tradition and also the establishment of a concept album tradition. Both can be laid at the feet of psychedelic music, which was considered more serious and artistic music, literally high-minded. When stoned, a band is prone to ponder and go on, and one is also prone to obsess on one topic. Ergo a confluence of album and concept album came to be demonstrated by the likes of the Beatles, Frank Zappa & the Mothers of Invention, The Kinks, The Who, Pretty Things and The Moody Blues.

And where does Yes fit in with all this, particularly pre-1970? Well, there's definitely a psychedelic element, but there's also a strong vocal group element, where Yes pick up on some of the more multi-vocal groups from the Haight-Ashbury scene, and down to Los Angeles. Because of Jon Anderson, the band's psychedelia is soft, tender, less dark and druggy than Steppenwolf, the Doors or Syd Barrett. And also because of Jon Anderson, strong vocal harmonies becomes a trademark of Yes, immediately, upon the

© Laurens Van Houten / Frank White Photo Agency

release of their self-titled debut album in 1969.

But there is also demonstration of a group that has strong instrumental ambitions, and herein lies Yes' usefulness in the story of progressive rock, even before they became the crowning example of the genre to be, beginning in the new decade. And surely, all the other bands credited with the birth of progressive rock pre-1970, including the Moody Blues, Pink Floyd, Jethro Tull, The Nice and Genesis—even Deep Purple—none of them are writing a full side of "Close to the Edge." In essence, given that progressive rock doesn't even exist yet, one might call these bands, variably, forms of studious and scholarly album rock, ambitiously adding their own biases, be they towards the blues, classical music, psych proper or hard rock.

Also, suddenly, as part of the pre-1970s story, we must note that the members of the first lineup of Yes, like the guys in Deep Purple and Led Zeppelin, had arrived there with some degree of resumé. We can include Rick Wakeman and Steve Howe in this phenomenon as well, with both quietly pushing the boundaries of their chosen instruments and for all the right reasons.

Bottom line, in terms of our story pre-1970, undoubtedly the main headline is that Yes had arrived with their debut album. And on that record, as I say, one is confronted with a curious mix of strong vocal work, instrumental discipline and good playing (but not wildly exploratory), new-agey hippie lightness of being, a bit of psych, a bit of fussy arrangement, bold tones, quite a bit of drama. This was a band that was going places, and that was a sentiment that could be gleaned simply from the seriousness in which the guys in the band addressed their career aspirations.

As we approach the end of the decade, it is hard not to view the closing four years of the '60s as providing what is possibly the most creatively explosive four-year run of musical and lyrical evolution that the rock 'n roll world has ever seen. And right at the end, there was little ol' Yes, with their own modest but accomplished and creditable contribution, placing their thumb print on the suddenly wall-filling canvas, with an idiosyncratic sound that would be a mere and rapidly discarded springboard to a wild, fantastic trip through aural Edens inconceivable to the most acid-unlocked hippie of the '60s. Yes had arrived with a polite wave, little aware that there was a ticking time bomb hiding behind their modest but likeable enough first record of comfortable conformity.

**June 31, 1944.** Artist Roger Dean is born, in Ashford, Kent. When one "sees" Yes, a fan is as likely to picture one of Roger's fantastic worlds created for them as he does live shots of the prog-rockers themselves.

**October 25, 1944.** John Roy "Jon" Anderson is born, Accrington, Lancashire, England, one of four children in the family. His father was a salesman and his mother worked in a cotton mill, and both were good ballroom dancers.

**January 11, 1945.** Anthony John "Tony Kaye" Selvidge is born in Leicester, England. Born into a musical family, Tony begins a lifelong study of the keyboards with piano lessons at the age of four. There's no indication as to how soon he began attacking the keyboard with his elbows.

**1946.** *Autobiography of a Yogi*, by Paramhansa Yoganada, is published by The Philosophical Library. A footnote on page 83 concerning the Shastric Scriptures will inspire Jon Anderson's lyrics for *Tales from Topographic Oceans*, and a subsequent lifetime of gentle ribbing over an album considered one of the most self-indulgent progressive rock farces of all time.

**September 29, 1946.** Ian Russell Wallace is born in Bury, Lancashire, England.

**April 8, 1947.** Stephen James "Steve" Howe is born in Holloway, North London, England, and brought up the youngest of four children.

**July 15, 1947.** Peter William "Peter Banks" Brockbanks is born, Barnet, North London.

**March 4, 1948.** Christopher Russell Edward "Chris" Squire, is born in Kingsbury, northwest London. His extensive experience as a trained choirboy through childhood will prove to be of career benefit later on, as will his early friendship with fellow songbird Andrew Pryce Jackman, who will become a musical collaborator in later years.

**June 24, 1948.** Patrick Philippe Moraz is born, in Morges, Switzerland.

**May 17, 1949.** William Scott "Bill" Bruford, is born in Sevenoaks, Kent, England.

**May 18, 1949.** Richard Christopher "Rick" Wakeman is born in Perivale, Middlesex, England.

**June 14, 1949.** Alan White is born in Pelton, County Durham, England.

**July 15, 1949.** Trevor Charles Horn is born in Hetton Le Hole, County Durham, England.

**August 25, 1952.** Geoffrey Downes is born, in Stockport, Cheshire, England.

**January 13, 1954.** Trevor Charles Rabin is born in Johannesburg, South Africa. Rabin would be instrumental in the reinvention of the band in and for the 1980s.

**1956.** Rick Wakeman begins piano lessons.

**1959.** Jon Anderson leaves school at 15 and takes a series of odd jobs, beginning as a farm hand and soon driving a truck. His father takes ill and it falls upon Jon and his older brother Tony to help support the family.

**1959.** Steve Howe receives, as a Christmas present, his first guitar; an f-hole acoustic. Steve hears for the first time artists who will become major inspirations such as Wes Montgomery and Chet Atkins.

**1961.** Steve acquires his first electric guitar, a solid body Guyatone; he is in his first group, with a regular gig playing Pentonville Prison twice a week. Meanwhile, Tony Kaye joins the Danny Rogers Orchestra, playing four shows a week. Alan White is given a set of Ajax drums, replaced within three months by a set of silver Ludwigs. Alan's uncle was a drummer and his dad was a piano player, with Alan taking piano lessons from the age of six.

**1962.** Jon Anderson joins The Warriors, sharing lead vocals with his brother Tony. Drummer for the band is Ian Wallace, later of King Crimson. The band cuts a single for Decca pairing "You Came Along" with "Don't Make Me Blue." Meanwhile, Alan White, who switched over to drums from piano, plays with his first band The Downbeats.

*Jon Anderson, on his musical brother:*
"Tony lives in the south of England now; he became a minister. But before, he was in the band… you remember that band that did the song 'Black is Black?' 'I want my baby back…' He went to join the Spanish band Los Bravos for a year, but he's changed direction and became interested in helping people and growing up with his family and became a priest."

*Ian Wallace:*
"The Warriors was my first foray into the dark nether regions of what is known as the music business. Jon Anderson was one of the singers in band along with his older brother, Tony. After Tony quit, the band spent about 18 months playing clubs in Germany and Denmark, six sets a night, every night and nine on weekends. After that I moved to Copenhagen and played for about six months with a soul band from Manchester called Big Sound. The remnants of Big Sound and The Warriors moved to London in 1968 and tried to make it there. Six of us lived in one room in the same house as some of Yes. I actually did a gig with Yes when their drummer at the time got sick, and they offered me the gig but I turned it down! I think I've remained friends with just about everyone I've worked with. Jon is definitely a good friend, but he tends to be rather elusive and I haven't seen or been in touch with him for some time."

**1963.** Rick Wakeman is in his first band, Atlantic Blues.

**1964.** Peter Banks, inspired first by Lonnie Donegan, then The Beatles and jazz guitarists like Wes Montgomery, is now past his first band The Nighthawks and into a new act called The Devil's Disciples, who cut a demo that is never commercially released.

**1964.** Steve gets himself a Gibson ES–175D, which will become a signature guitar for the future Yes man. Same year, Steve records for the first time, a cover of Chuck Berry's "Maybelline," with his Joe Meek-produced band The Syndicats. Two more singles, "Howling for My Baby" and "On the Horizon," would follow, before Steve would move on to The In Crowd.

Tomorrow in July 1967; from left: Steve Howe, John Alder, John Wood.

**1964.** His dreams ignited by The Beatles, Chris Squire is suspended from Haberdashers' Aske's Boys' School for his long hair. His first group, The Selfs compete in a battle of the bands, only to be beaten out by The Bo Street Runners.

**1965.** A young Roger Dean, after living all over the world with his family, is now back in the UK and enrolling at The Royal College of Art.

**1965.** Tony Kaye adds to his resume, having now played with Johnny Taylor's Star Combo, The Federals and Roy Orbison. Meanwhile Alan, already gigging since the age of 13 and gaining accolades as "the youngest drummer in England," wins a battle of the bands with his act The Blue Chips, the name recently changed from The Downbeats.

**1965.** Chris Squire puts aside his Futurama bass and gets his first Rickenbacker 4001, an instrument only a year old in terms of its invention. Squire will go on to become one of Rickenbacker's greatest ambassadors. He is now in his second group, The Syn (no relation to The Syndicats). Chris is soon joined by future Yes guitarist Peter Banks.

> *Peter Banks:*
> *"I met Chris Squire on Denmark Street through a drummer friend that I knew named Martin Adelman. It turned out that Martin was the drummer in this band called The Syn, and Chris was the bassist in the group as well. As fate would have it, they just so happened to be looking for a guitar player. It all happened really quickly. They said, 'Come into our manager's office,' which was also on Denmark Street. The Syn had another guitar player at the time named Jon Painter, and this was my first introduction to how cold the music business could be. Because I remember meeting the rest of the band, maybe two or three days later, and they said, 'We want to get rid of our guitar player, so why don't you come along and watch us play?' And that's exactly what I did. I went to see them on maybe three or four gigs, and even got to know the guitar player and his girlfriend. To be honest, he was a very nice guy. Yet the whole time I'm watching him, I full well knew that I was eventually going to replace him in The Syn."*

**April 1965.** Parlophone issue a single by Steve Howe's band The In Crowd, pairing Otis Redding's "That's How Strong My Love Is" with "Things She Says." The single goes to No.48 on the UK charts. Two more singles follow in the fall, "Stop, Wait a Minute"/"You're on Your Own" and "Why Must They Criticise"/"I Don't Mind," before the band change their name to Tomorrow.

**1966.** Steve's band Tomorrow, play two songs, "Am I Glad to See You" and "Blow-up" in the movie *Blow-Up*.

**1966.** Rick Wakeman is in The Concordes, later called the Concord Quartet, with Rick soon acquiring his first electronic instrument, a Pianet. Meanwhile, down in South Africa, Trevor Rabin switches from piano to guitar and forms a group called Conglomeration.

**1966.** Bill Bruford is in a group called The Breed, followed by The Noise in 1967 and Savoy Brown in 1968, although he only plays three shows with that band.

**1967.** Steve, still in Tomorrow, appears in a pie fight scene in a comedy about the Mod movement called *Smashing Time*. Trevor Rabin has moved on from Conglomeration to Freedom's Children to Rabbitt.

From left: John Wood, John Alder, Keith West, Steve How.

**May 1967.** Tomorrow issue their first single, "My White Bicycle"/"Claramount Lake," on Parlophone. A cover of the A-side would become a minor hit for Nazareth in 1975. Meanwhile, the band is recording what will become their debut album, with Mark P. Wirtz producing.

**June 1, 1967.** The Beatles' *Sgt. Pepper's Lonely Hearts Club Band* is issued. The album is considered one of the early examples of a concept album, although the degree to which the record is conceptual has been hotly debated ever since its splashy entry into the world.

**June 23, 1967.** Chris Squire's and Peter Banks' group, The Syn (Mk I) issue, on Deram, "Created by Clive"/"Grounded." Chris likens The Syn very much to Yes, given its five-man lineup and emphasis on vocal harmonies.

**August 1967.** The Warriors, after a brief German tour, break up in Frankfurt, Jon having been left to lead vocals after the departure of his brother Tony back at the end of 1965.

> *Jon Anderson on making ends meet as a young rock 'n' roller:*
> "Thanks to working as a lorry driver, I found The Cavern. I was driving in Liverpool delivering sugar and flowers, and then I drove around the corner and saw The Cavern where The Beatles started, and about six years later I was playing there!"

**August 5, 1967.** Pink Floyd issue their debut album, *The Piper at the Gates of Dawn*, and the progressive rock era is born, even though the band is essentially a psychedelic rock band at this point.

**September 1967.** Tomorrow issue their second single, "Revolution"/"Three Jolly Little Dwarves."

**September 1, 1967.** The Syn (Mk II) issue, again on Deram, their second single "Flowerman"/"14th Hour Technicolor Dream," in a picture sleeve. Chris cites The Syn supporting Jimi Hendrix at the Marquee as one of his pre-Yes career highlights.

**September 21, 1967.** The very first John Peel show session, on BBC Radio One, features Steve Howe's band, Tomorrow.

**Late 1967.** Chris Squire has the mother of bad acid trips, which turns him into a recluse for a few months as he sorts his head out. The silver lining is that throughout the process of coming down, he woodsheds heavily with his bass guitar.

**November 1967.** Although many records could be said to be the first concept album, and for different reasons, *Days of Future Past*, issued by The Moody Blues this month, is arguably the first concept album by a progressive rock band. Of note, Yes, although squarely a progressive rock band, rarely wrote in the concept album format, with 1974's *Tales from Topographic Oceans* being the only clear-cut example.

**1968.** Steve Howe marries Jan, still his wife today. The couple had four children, although, tragically, their musician son Virgil died of a heart attack in 2017 at the age of 41.

**1968.** Geoff Downes gets his first Hammond organ, at the age of 16.

**January 1968.** Chris Squire forms Mabel Greer's Toyshop, after The Syn cease operation at the end of 1967, disappointed at failing to find a record deal, and simultaneously handicapped by Chris' LSD overdose and the fact that the band's lead singer wanted to hang it up, get married and get into the fashion business.

**February 1968.** Tomorrow issue their self-titled debut album.

**March 1968.** Parlophone issues a Jon Anderson demo as a single. The track, released under the pseudonym Hans Christian, is a cover of "Never My Love" by The Association.

**March 1968.** Chris Squire gets Peter Banks into his psychedelic group Mabel Greer's Toyshop. Jon Anderson is soon inserted into the group as Peter Banks leaves to join Neat Change, Banks managing to record the B-side of a single with them over his six-month stay. While Peter is away, guitarist in the band is Clive Bailey.

*Jon Anderson:*
"When you're first in a band, you copy the stuff you like. When I was in my first band, we copied the Beatles and the Rolling Stones, and then we copied the Beach Boys and Frank Zappa. There was that band called Vanilla Fudge, and we copied them a bit. But eventually, you start finding your own way."

*Peter Banks:*
"I remember one gig where Mabel Greer's Toyshop played for an encore 'In the Midnight Hour' which went on for about 30 minutes. Well, this little guy came up on stage and sang with us. It turns out this guy was none other than Jon Anderson. I didn't know Jon then, but Chris did, so he must've invited him up to sing with the group. Ironically, Bill Bruford had also sat in with Mabel Greer's Toyshop at a gig at the Rachel McMillen College in London. But I didn't really know Bill either. This particular gig is so often mentioned in 'Yes-lore.' I'm not really sure if I was there or not. It's hard to remember some things."

"One thing's for sure, Mabel Greer's Toyshop rehearsed a lot more than they gigged, which is not a good sign. We were not a band like The Syn. We were not touring up and down the country in a van. Mabel Greer never toured. We just played one or two gigs a week and that was about it. I finally had enough of that group after six months or so. Although I do believe they did continue for a while after I left. I then joined another band called the Neat Change, which is basically a Skinhead-type of group, the antithesis of Mabel Greer."

**May 1968.** A second Hans Christian single, called "(The Autobiography of) Mississippi Hobo," is issued by Parlophone.

**May 1968.** Steve Howe is now in a band called Bodast, who garner interest from Deep Purple's US label Tetragrammaton, recording a number of tracks for a proposed debut album. But the company goes bankrupt before an album could be realised. Cast adrift, Steve joins The Nice (for a day!) and is rumoured for the Jethro Tull gig.

**Early June 1968.** Drummer for Mabel Greer's Toyshop, Bob Hagger, is replaced by Bill Bruford. Bruford, torn between his economic studies at Leeds University and a career in music, hitchhikes home to England with his drum set after a disastrous run in Italy with a band called The Noise. His ad in the *Melody Maker* looking for drumming work is answered by Jon Anderson.

**June 7, 1968.** Bill Bruford plays his first show with Mabel Greer's Toyshop, at Deptford College.

**Summer 1968.** An attempt is made to pair Jon Anderson with the Gurvitz brothers group, The Gun. A showcase gig takes place, but the favourable response to the show is dampened when Jon is sacked shortly after.

*Jon Anderson:*
"They fired me! Adrian Gurvitz and the guys were really nice and we got on well. We'd only practised for three weeks before a show at Middle Earth, but we went down well. Then we played the Marquee for free with The Who, which I thought was wonderful, just to get seen. But afterwards they said, 'Where's the money for the petrol?' Of course, there wasn't any. They got very uptight and a week later, I saw them advertised for a show and they'd forgotten to tell me!"

**July 1968.** Mabel Greer's Toyshop invite Tony Kaye, recently of Bittersweet and Winston's Fumbs, to join the group. Returned by this point is Peter Banks, previously of The Syn but also an earlier version of Mabel Greer's Toyshop, before his six month defection to Neat Change. The guys—in order of arrival to the ranks: Chris Squire, Jon Anderson, Bill Bruford, Peter Banks, Tony Kaye—are now set on acquiring a new name, frontrunners being Life and Yes. A handful of gigs take place throughout July although these are not considered official Yes gigs.

*Peter Banks:*
"It was me who came up with the name Yes. Actually, a couple years before, around the time of The Syn, I had the name floating around. I always liked one word names and Yes was short and sweet—it looked big on posters. Since it was only three letters, it would get printed bigger, like The Who. The name must've stuck with Chris, because he and Jon decided to call the group that at the beginning. Believe it or not, the name was supposed to be only temporary. The group figured we'd come up with a better name later—that was the idea. Like all names, at first, it sounded a little silly and a little pretentious. Yet after six months it kind of stuck and nobody came up with something better, so Yes was it."

**August 3, 1968.** Yes play their first show as Yes at a campsite, East Mersey Youth Camp in Essex, followed by a show on the 5th at the Marquee in London.

**September 16, 1968.** Trial by fire, Yes play a gig in place of the last-minute no-show Sly & The Family Stone. Going on at 1:00 AM, the band won over the surprised crowd, which included the likes of Eric Clapton, Pete Townsend and Jimi Hendrix. This show was also where the band met their first manager Roy Flynn, who was also in charge of the venue. Flynn now takes over from Jack Barrie and quickly proves his mettle, securing the band better gigs and culminating in getting the band signed with the prestigious Atlantic label.

The same month Bill Bruford quit the band to study at Leeds University. He is replaced by Tony O'Reilly who struggles to perform with the group and after a disastrous gig, Yes begged Bill to come back, which he did.

*Chris Squire:*
"There was somebody there who suggested to the club manager that they get us, because we lived really close to the club and had all our equipment readily available. I was actually in bed at the time! We got organised and went out and played. There were a lot of stars there at the time. The members of the Beatles were there. At the end of the night, the manager of the club was so relieved that he offered to manage us. It probably wasn't the greatest thing that ever happened to him in his life (laughs)."

**November 1969 - January 1970.** Yes work on their second album, again at Advision Studios, London, with producer Tony Colton.

*Peter Banks:*
*"Eddie Offord did the engineering, and did an incredible job considering what he had put up with. There's an interesting story about how we ended up with Eddie Offord as the engineer. I remember Bill and I were listening to John McLaughlin's first solo album, called* Extrapolation. *I think I played it for Bill, and he was totally knocked out by the drum sound, particularly the bass sound. Because the bass was just an acoustic bass, but it was so far up in the mix. Certainly no one in the jazz field had ever recorded jazz like that. So Bill and I wondered, 'Who produced this?' Well, lo and behold, the album was produced by Eddie Offord. We both thought, 'Who the hell is this guy?' Ironically, it turned out that Eddie worked at Advision Studios! So Eddie just kind of came along with the studio."*

*"I believe* Extrapolation *was the first album he had ever produced. And Bill and I just loved it. Bill and I went into this second album very much with the idea of the* Extrapolation *album, with Yes sounding like that, especially in the bass drum department. Of course, it turned out very differently. Eddie Offord was a real character. He had great ears, fantastic ears! He was very proficient, but not particularly technical. And he was very good at all the tricks in the studio. I've never seen anybody on a mixing board like Eddie before. He was very cool, and used to get very stoned and sometimes become incomprehensible. He and Jon took an instant bonding, and there would be lots of intense conversations at four in the morning, leaning on the faders. It was that type of atmosphere. It's really a shame that he didn't produce the second Yes record; Tony Colton, the producer, on the other hand was a whole different package. Let's face it, he hated me—it's as simple as that."*

**November 26 - December 2, 1969.** Yes play five dates in Switzerland. November 30th finds the band on a bill with Deep Purple, Brian Auger and the Trinity, Manfred Mann, Free, Atomic Rooster, Liverpool Scene and Village.

**December 12, 1969.** The Plastic, Ono Band, featuring John Lennon and Yoko Ono, issue a live album called *Live Peace in Toronto 1969*. The band's drummer is Alan White, who plays with John on and off over a two-year period. Pre-Yes, Alan would also play with Billy Fury and the Gamblers, Ginger Baker's Airforce, Balls, Bell + Arc (supporting The Who in the US), Happy Magazine (later called Griffin), and for a year-and-a-half, Alan Price.

Switzerland, 1969.

Peter Banks performing at Bristol University's Anson Rooms on 4th October 1969.

"Jazz and rock are quite different. Rock is generally slow and loud. Jazz, generally speaking, is fast and light. Rock, generally speaking, is played pretty much all the way through with one pattern. Jazz, as you know, is improvised. In other words, they couldn't be more different. All the great jazz drummers I know play quite quietly and are trying to play quieter. Most of the rock drummers play loud and are trying to play louder. Everything is probably about as different as it can get. Jazz tends to take place in small, intimate rooms where the speed of the playing and the excitement of it can translate well to 300 to 500 people, that kind of number."

"Rock of course takes place in stadiums where, if you are in the back of the hall, you need to wait a week before you hear anything. I grew up with jazz as a kid. From 13 to 18, 19, it had been the love of my life. And I knew how to play jazz better than I knew how to play rock when I joined Yes. Not that any of us thought much about rock or jazz. We just kind of started playing. If you asked me at the time and forced me, I would've said that I thought Yes was going to be a jazz group. I didn't know it was going to be a rock group. That didn't matter. It just changed direction a bit."

**Bill Bruford**

# 1970: Time and a Word

© Laurens Van Houten / Frank White Photo Agency

The 1970s, for Yes, is the story of an improbable band of nerdy types operating collectively at a surreal level, in a music industry that resembles not a wit the one we have today. The band begins the decade sputtering, not happy with their label, not getting anywhere with their second album, *Time and a Word*, despite its pretty daunting prog rock appointments. And yet, eccentric ignorer of accepted tone values Steve Howe replaces Peter Banks on guitar (in fact three months before *Time and a Word* hits the shops), and possibilities expand two- and three- and four-fold.

Still, 1970 finds the band progressing, playing gigs, and demonstrating a propensity toward grandiosity, through Jon Anderson's increasingly mystical lyrics on the record as well as the incorporation of orchestra, which proved to be the key point of contention with Banks, resulting in his ouster.

What's almost more important about 1970 in the life of at least the milieu of Yes is that the year marked the birth of progressive rock writ large—with Yes not quite there and arguably falling back. Jethro Tull were already onto their third album *Benefit*, while Van der Graaf Generator issued their defining second and third albums, Genesis, their defining second album. High up the ladder creatively and fearlessly, King Crimson bound in and confounded with a pair of perplexing records. The year also saw albums by the likes of Magma, Family, Traffic, The Moody Blues, Pink Floyd, Procol Harum, The Nice, Soft Machine, Gong, Amon Düül II, Colosseum, Caravan, Cressida and Curved Air, not to mention debuts by Gentle Giant and Emerson, Lake & Palmer.

A momentous 1971 for Yes would erase any doubts about the band's ability to compete, but for now, Yes was still working on wrapping up their Deep Purple Mk I phase as it were, while a new progressive rock scene exploded in close vicinity around them.

**HAROLD DAVISON & MARQUEE-BLOCK PRESENT**

**YES**

IN CONCERT

**QUEEN ELIZABETH HALL - LONDON**

(Adjacent to the Royal Festival Hall)

**THIS SATURDAY, 21st MARCH, 7.45 p.m.**

"Yes" will be joined this evening by the twenty-piece orchestra, who accompany them on certain tracks of their new Album, "Time and a Word", to be released shortly on Atlantic Records.

Tickets: 8/-, 10/-, 14/-, 17/-, 21/-

Available from Royal Festival Hall Box Office, all usual agents and Harold Davison Ltd., 235-241 Regent Street, London, W.1.

**1970.** Jon Anderson marries Jennifer; their marriage would last 25 years and produce three children. Also in 1970, Rick Wakeman marries for the first time. Divorcing Roz Woolford in 1980, the union produced three children: sons Oliver, Adam and Benjamin; the couple also raised stepdaughter Amanda.

**January 30, 1970.** A particularly top-notch bill finds Yes playing Lanchester University, Coventry along with Atomic Rooster, Free and Mott the Hoople.

**February 19 – 24, 1970.** Yes play Scandinavian dates with the Edgar Broughton Band, following upon three shows earlier in the month with The Nice.

**March 21, 1970.** Yes play a rushed, haphazard second set of a concert with orchestra, at Queen Elizabeth Theatre, conducted by Tony Cox. The orchestra consisted of students from the Royal School of Music. Peter Banks was against orchestra being used for the album, and he was against doing this type of gig, an idea of Jon's.

**April 1970.** Rick Wakeman joins The Strawbs.

**April 18, 1970.** Peter Banks plays his last gig with Yes, after which Steve Howe joins as his replacement, Robert Fripp having turned the gig down. With much tension between Banks and producer Tony Colton, it had been pretty much decided during the close of the sessions for the album, interspersed with steady gigging, that Peter would have to go.

*Peter Banks:*
"I got fired from Yes after a gig in my home county in Hertfordshire, at Luton College. I don't think it was a particularly bad gig, and I don't think it was a particularly great one. After the show in the dressing room, I was given the news. Jon was the one who broke it to me, and Chris was there also. Actually, Tony and Bill didn't even know about it until that day, which I found out later. Jon said to me, 'I think it would be better for you and the band if you left. And the reason is…' At that point I went crazy and yelled, 'Don't give me any fucking reasons!' I didn't want to know. I guess I was kind of in a state of shock."

"And so I just packed up my little gig bag. The worst thing was that I couldn't even storm off and leave, which would've been the sensible thing to do, because we all drove to the gig in the same car. So I had to hang around and drive back with them to London, or I'd have been stuck there. The drive home was very uncomfortable. I didn't say anything and nobody else did either, because I was obviously very upset. I was extremely angry! Frankly, I think if anybody would've said something, I probably would've punched them. I made that totally clear. It was a total shock to me, a complete surprise. I had no idea at all that I was going to be fired from the band that I loved! And as I found out later, neither did Bill or Tony."

*Steve Howe:*
"When I went for the audition for Yes it was quite a straightforward thing. I had been putting my face around saying, 'I am not doing anything right now.' That was about the most time I have ever been without a group when I wanted to be in a group. Chris called and said, 'We have been seeing you play and you have been doing great things. Come and see what it is like to play with us.' It was that first day that I heard in Jon and Chris tremendous originality, capability, style and technique. Bill was just awesome. When Bill played I was like, 'I think I'm going to like this!'"

"I didn't really start playing an instrument until I was 27, 28, when I started playing piano and guitar at home. But it was very lame at the start, and then I met Vangelis who was a mentor for me. I used to watch what he played and how he played. Then I got home and tried to be a 'sort of Vangelis.' It's impossible but I was trying to imitate his work and learn more about technology. And now I have a very beautiful studio; I have some very fine equipment, so I can compose every day, some symphony or some other music. Over the years you grow into your own style."
**Jon Anderson**

# 1971: The Yes Album and Fragile

© Laurens Van Houten / Frank White Photo Agency

The *Yes Album* is such a conundrum, yet it triumphs. People begin talking about this strange band of holdover hippies, rescuing then bending psychedelic rock in a scholarly manner until a maturing progressive rock idiom is addressed. All wiry and lanky, extended and ethereal, the band's songs break all the rules, and the wheel with spokes that is nascent progressive rock fans out to new territory. Each member of the band can he heard and divined to distinction, but it is Tony Kaye with his forceful Hammond work that distinguishes the band, broadly speaking, at the nexus between *The Yes Album* and what came after.

Next plot twist, through the bloody-minded insistence represented by following four flag-plant albums, the centre shifts for the definition of prog rock, to the place that Yes resides. To be sure, there would be other fiefdoms, but when the collective rock subconscious thinks prog rock without additional qualifiers or descriptives, the answer is Yes. The takeover of what prog means begins with *The Yes Album* but is underscored by *Fragile*, also, shockingly issued in 1971, wherein another enabler of the fantastical joins the band, namely hotshot keyboardist about town, Rick Wakeman. A song pulsating upon the bed of Bill Bruford's and Chris Squire's ingenious rhythm track called "Roundabout" is edited down for single consumption, and Yes is off to the races, infecting, informing.

In the UK, the rock music of the day also now consists of nascent glam, strong openers for heavy metal, still much retrograde rock 'n' roll, and in general, the continuing category known vaguely as album rock. But there's also now a subset of that called symphonic rock, art rock, progressive rock or even jazz rock, which is essentially a dressing-up of underground rock, carrying on from Cream through the poorly selling—save for Heep and Sabbath—Vertigo Records ethic. It's a murky melange of music that, on paper, shouldn't sell, but weirdly does so anyway. In 1971, Yes is at the vortex of all of it, creating two career-defining albums that set the stage for a fairly plush commercial recline that would last certainly through to about 1979.

© Laurens Van Houten / Frank White Photo Agency

**1971.** "Yours Is No Disgrace" is issued as a single, but only on the mainland.

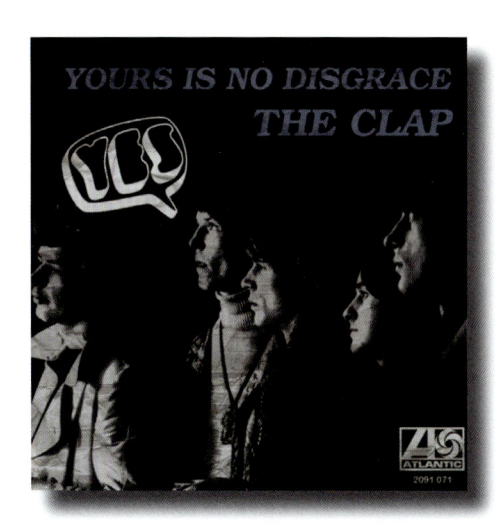

*Jon Anderson, in 1977:*
*"I've enjoyed having a hit single. We were on Top of the Pops many years ago when 'Yours Is No Disgrace' was released. But it was a horrible experience. It was like being on a production line. You were shunted into a small dressing room and then put on a stage. Producing a video film for a show is much better from our point of view."*

**January 8, 1971.** Yes begin an extensive tour of mainland Europe supporting Iron Butterfly. The bands get along great, jamming into the night. Yes is hugely impressed with the American band's modern and sophisticated PA system and vow to get one of their own, winding up buying Iron Butterfly's, given that the band was in the process of breaking up. Management and Atlantic's Phil Carson conspire to finance the equipment, but in the process, Yes cede some of their publishing monies to their management company.

**January 16, 1971.** Future Yes vocalist Jon Davison, is born.

**Early 1971.** Patrick Moraz's progressive rock band Mainhorse issue their only album, a self-titled, on Polydor.

**Early 1971.** Osibisa issue their debut self-titled album. An as yet undiscovered Roger Dean is the cover artist of choice, Dean also illustrating the band's follow-up, *Woyaya*, issued the same year, in his signature style. It is his Osibisa work that Yes had seen, prompting a call to Roger from Steve.

**March 5, 1971.** "Your Move" is issued as a US single from *The Yes Album*, backed with "The Clap." The single reaches No.40 on the charts.

**March 19, 1971.** Yes issue their third record, *The Yes Album*. The band hang onto their Atlantic deal when Phil Carson convinces Ahmet Ertegun to rescind his notice to drop Yes from the label. The album would reach No.40 in the US and No.4 in the UK, a lofty position that Chris attributes to a British postal strike—sales results to be tabulated were limited to the Virgin store in London, where the band's fan base was strongest.

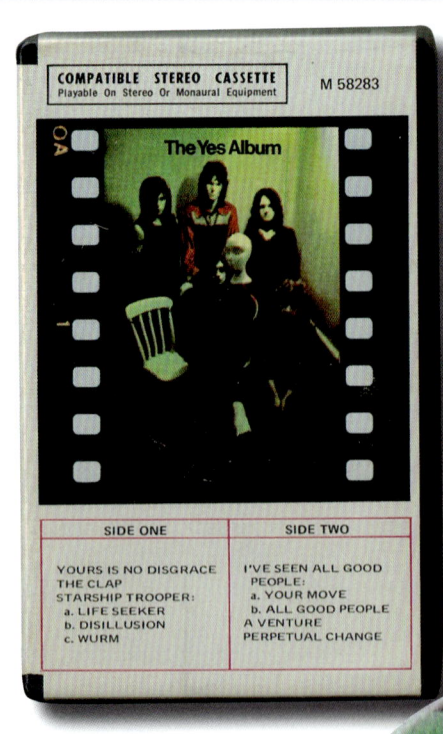

Bill Bruford performing at the Crystal Palace Garden Party at the Crystal Palace Bowl, 31st July 1971. Yes was second on the bill to Elton John.

### Chris Squire:

"Remember, this was very much the era of the album being the important part. The single thing was secondary, really, in that era. All of us were a bit surprised that Atlantic Records wanted to cut down 'Roundabout' to make it more palatable at radio, to make it a kind of digestible piece of music. We went along with it, but we weren't really happy with the edit, which was done with some Atlantic engineer in New York. We didn't think it was a very good edit, but it went out anyway, and of course, now lots of people have heard it (laughs). Ultimately it was a good thing, but we weren't really focused on singles."

### Jon Anderson on the silver lining around the "Roundabout" edit:

"It was very simple, basically. When we put together the Fragile album, that was the real testing ground for us as a band. We had written, together, 'Heart of the Sunrise' and 'Starship Trooper' and these are long-form pieces, you know? Especially 'Heart of the Sunrise;' very complicated piece. And it's one of those things, if you'd have been in the studio when we did it, there I was with a very, very simple song idea, and Chris and Steve and Bill were doing this sort of aggressive phrasing. And I just walk over and say, 'Can you do that in another key?' and they did. And, 'Can you do it in another key?' and they did. And I said, 'Great, because that could be the beginning, and then the song will come.' And that's how it worked. I'd be listening to what people were doing and performing, and sort of drag it into the complex idea. And that was the concept of making music."

"So at that time, as it happened, we toured in America, with the Fragile album. See, Fragile and Close to the Edge were actually done in the same year, which is quite a trip. Musically speaking, it's an incredible amount of music, and I think it's because we were very connected. We were very much in harmony. And what you had was, we started playing around America and Canada, and we were starting to play universities. And the local radio stations, the university radio stations, were actually working with FM, for the first time, which is a higher frequency and actually didn't have many advertisements in their daily projection of music. So when we went to these radio stations, they would play the whole of 'Roundabout,' which was kind of wonderful to us, because that's how it was created."

"But 'Roundabout' was also edited down to a five-minute single, without us knowing. And it was a big surprise to hear it on the radio. And of course, we were very musically zealous and said, oh, why did you get the big scissors out and do that? But of course, it became a very big hit record, and that's why we sold a million records. It wasn't because of the long-form pieces. 'Roundabout' made us into a commercial entity, which was very interesting, because you had, say, a million people buying the record, and they would come and see the show, and go, 'What the heck is this?' (laughs). Expecting us to do ten versions of 'Roundabout,' or that kind of song, kind of a nice and dance-y and poppy kind of song. Which is cool, but that wasn't all we were. And so that's why we gained these legions of fans, which were very connected to what we were doing. And the reason was that we were connected to what we were doing. We weren't doing it just to be rock stars."

### Bill Bruford:

"The Yes Album I don't remember so much about. We were still in our Beatles phase I think, writing Beatles-influenced songs, on that album. But Fragile, that was a bit of a misconception, in a way. 'Heart of the Sunrise' was great, 'Roundabout' was great, but the general mood within the band was one of frustration. And I remember distinctly suggesting that we all—any one of us—could write music for the group and should so do, and everybody should be given one track with which to use the talents of the group, write something for the group, and orchestrate it the way they wanted to. That fell into a big mistake and turned into a solo track by Howe, a solo track by Wakeman, and I think Jon and I were the only ones who managed to write something for the group."

**December 17, 1971.** Rick Wakeman plays on David Bowie's fourth album, *Hunky Dory*.

*Rick Wakeman:*
"I was very lucky with that album; I'd worked with David on 'Space Oddity' and I did 'Memory of a Free Festival' and 'Wild Eyed Boy from Freecloud' with him, and then he called me 'round his house and said, 'I want to play you some songs,' and he played me 'Life on Mars?' on this battered 12-string, that phenomenal song, and my jaw dropped. He said, 'On the album, I want it to come from the piano, not from the acoustic guitar. So I want you to make some notes, learn the song and then play it almost as a piano solo, and I would get the band and everybody to work around what you do,' which was wonderful. Some people have said, 'You must've worked really hard to do that arrangement,' but it was actually very easy 'cause everybody had to work around me."

"The worst thing about *Close to the Edge* is that at the end of it Bill said, 'I'm leaving' (laughs). And I was totally devastated. I mean, I couldn't believe that Bill had even been thinking of it. I love Bill very much; he's a friend of mine. But I couldn't believe it. I mean, he knows I was obviously so shocked. I was almost… well, I was upset. Because I didn't want Bill to leave. I had no desire for Bill to go at all. And the fact that he wanted to go with Fripp also tended to insult me more, because he was a guitarist. It was a bit like me deciding to go with Aynsley Dunbar, or I was gonna join a band with Stewart Copeland. 'Bill, I'm gonna join a band with Stewart Copeland— goodbye!' And Bill said to me, 'I'm gonna join a band, and it's called King Crimson,' and I knew that was Robert Fripp."

"But I also understood and respected greatly Bill's musicality, and his desire to learn about music, which is why he went to Fripp. He wanted to learn more about improvising, more about free music. And he considered *Close to the Edge* actually quite commercial (laughs). Well, I mean, in record sales it has to be. It has to have been seen in some way as being commercial. But commercial because it's uncommercial, more than it's commercial because it repeats the main line 25 times."
**Steve Howe**

# 1972: Close to the Edge

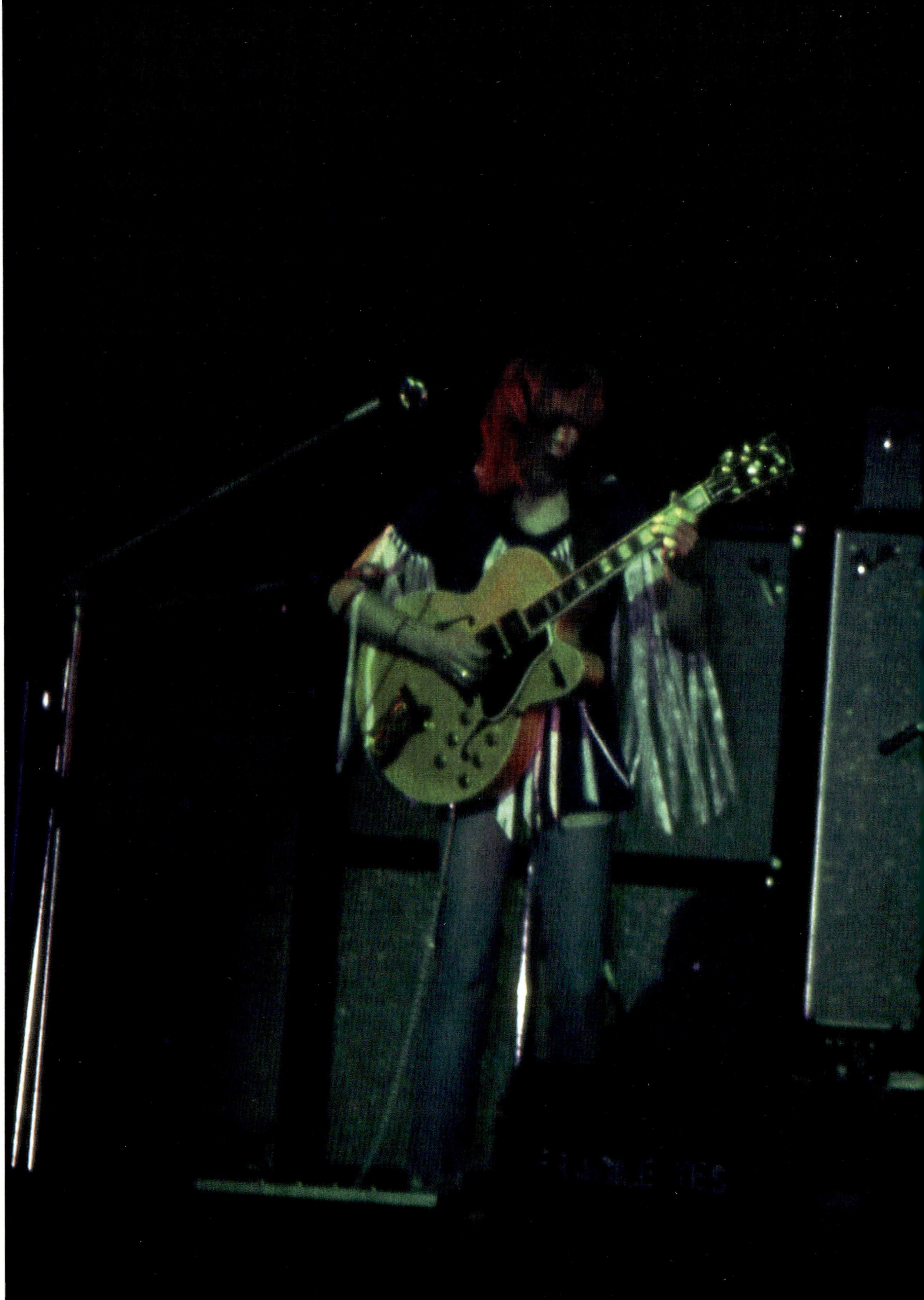

© Jim Kozlowski / Frank White Photo Agency

© Jim Kozlowski / Frank White Photo Agency

75

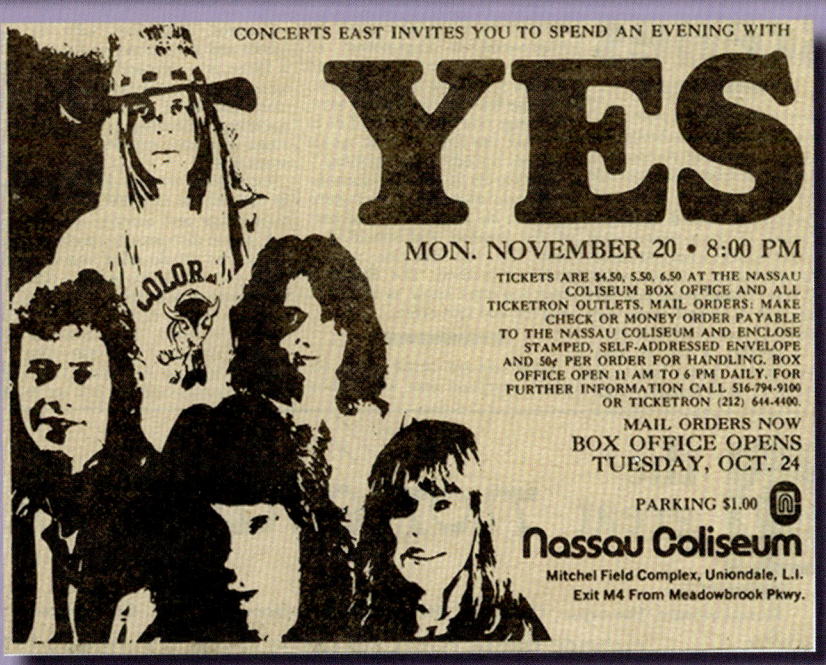

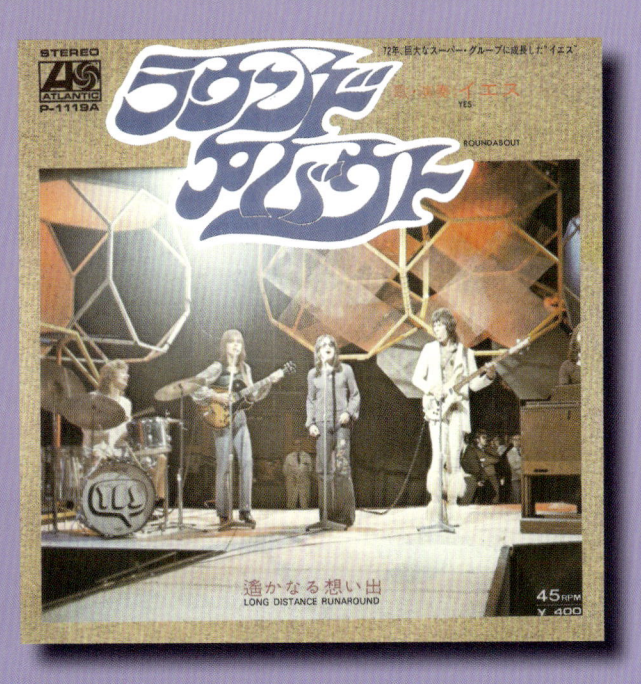

**November 1972.** Flash issue their second album, *In the Can*, rush-finished after the band returned from their first US tour, September 18, 1972.

> **Author review:**
> "This post-Yes Peter Banks vehicle was a not-to-be-ridiculed marriage between pop and progressive, Flash also adding elements of Wishbone Ash-like leads and faint proto-metal from years gone by. But mainly what we have here is complex, involved song structures not over-laden with chops, sorta like soundtrack or stage music, passage leading to passage to passage, each part on its own not all that remarkable. Sorta Tull, Genesis, Gentle Giant and moldy Yes all mushed together, In the Can is a disciplined enough hippie excursion, even lightening up for a 1:50 drum solo called 'Stop That Banging.' Vocalist Colin Carter is perhaps a bit of an old '60s ham, but one can become endeared. All in all, In the Can shows its age, sounding not unlike Banks-era Yes stretched out to prog extremes."

**December 1972.** Chris Squire buys a home called New Pipers (situated in Virginia Water, Surrey), which the band will take advantage of for recording purposes. Also in '72, he marries Nikki, entering into his first of three marriages. Chris tells the story how he went from renting a flat to buying a mansion with no steps in-between; similarly, his first car was a Bentley.

**December 26, 1972.** The band's warehouse in Willesden is broken in to. Pieces of equipment stolen include three amplifiers, a lighting control panel, Gibson pedal boards and two Minimoogs.

January 21st, 1972, Rotterdam, Netherlands. Show began at 12:15 on the night of January 20th, therefore correct date is January 21st.

A NEW ALBUM

"One attitude I have towards playing, is that when I was young—I guess it's because I'm a Gemini—I liked lots of different kinds of music, from classical to jazz, big band, fusion, R&B and rock 'n' roll. I was a big Weather Report fan from when I was 18. So I try to incorporate that all into one style, but I want to always play with a lot of feel to it. One of my philosophies in playing, though, is just to play what is necessary for the songs. And wherever there is a possibility to try and do something different—we play things in fives and sevens, and it's pretty complex—that makes for some interesting drum playing beneath the melodies. There's so many people that play so many different ways. I like the Steve Smiths of the world, Lenny White; some of the fusion guys I loved a lot, and I use things from them within my style. Andy Newmark, Steve Gadd—all those guys influenced me from a distance in different ways."
Alan White

# 1973: Tales from Topographic Oceans

© Laurens Van Houten / Frank White Photo Agency

Enter 1973 and Yes had major ambitions, including the invention of punk rock. Through their preposterously indulgent, noodling, inscrutably hippie-fried and spiritual *Tales from Topographic Oceans* album from the winter of 1973, a quiet revolt had begun, where the rock audience was becoming not so much fed-up en masse, but fragmented, with more than enough still patronizing rock bombast in droves, but also a sizable amount revolting at the rock star excess, the self-importance, and the sheer expense all around of the extreme progressive lunacy that Yes was practising. *Tales from Topographic Oceans*, not much more mainstream than a record financed by the Krishnas or the Moonies, became a lightning rod, a signifier that hippies must take their depleting numbers off the streets once and for all and pixie-dance into the fields and forests where they belong.

And so it became that any time journalists and punk rockers themselves talked about why punk rock had to happen, the near impermeable *Tales from Topographic Oceans* is usually cited as the one record that was a bridge too far. Next we would hear about huge British bands like Led Zeppelin and Deep Purple spending all their time touring America and rarely playing at home. Next would be a description of the ridiculousness that was Emerson, Lake & Palmer live. And then if anyone was still listening, there'd be a denigration of bands turning three-minute songs into 15-minute renditions on stage, through gratuitous jamming and soloing. But if there's one foggy record that gets blamed for the Sex Pistols, Clash and The Damned, it's *Tales from Topographic Oceans*, and for that accomplishment, we salute the heroes of this book ('cos in actual fact I love two of those bands more than I love Yes).

© Laurens Van Houten / Frank White Photo Agency

**1973.** Roy Flynn, manager of the band through the *Time and a Word* era, settles out of court with subsequent management company Hemdale (personified by Brian Lane) for $150,000, in payment for his considerable investment keeping the band afloat in the lean years.

**January 23, 1973.** Rick Wakeman issues his first of what will become over 100 solo albums, *The Six Wives of Henry VIII*—a 1971 covers record called *Piano Vibrations* is alternately considered the first, but not by Rick and many Yes fans. The album reaches No.30 on Billboard and goes gold. Guesting on the record are Yes alumni Steve Howe, Chris Squire, Bill Bruford and Alan White, with "Catherine of Aragon" turning out to be pretty much a Yes track without Jon Anderson.

### Rick Wakeman on his songwriting, particularly on piano:

"I can thank David Bowie very much, because David told me many years ago to write everything on the piano. He said, 'If you write it on the piano and it works as a piece of music, you can do anything with it.' He writes everything on a really horrible old 12-string guitar, and he says, 'If it sounds good on this, then I know it will sound good whatever I do; it can only get better and better and better.' And so everything that I've ever written, I've done on the piano, and the great thing about that is that you can't get any more minimalistic than when you're sitting at the piano."

### Author review:

"One of the key, most popular Wakeman records of the man's vast catalogue of approximately a hundred titles, The Six Wives is a pleasant enough marriage of progressive rock and renaissance classical, Wakeman overflowing with every sort of keyboard sound from then-modern synth to pipe organ. Reinforcing each daunting track is a coterie of players, most notable performances coming from the bass players and drummers, both guitars and vocals (used instrumentally) left merely textural, as keyboards, bass and drums propel most tracks to blustery, dreamy conclusions. The record is designed to instrumentally evoke the temperament of the six wives, each partitioned to a track, each supported on the back cover with a short paragraph of biography. Picture instrumental Yes or Jethro Tull super-dosed with keyboards and you'll pretty much arrive at this melancholy, often mysterious and depressing affair. Laid the groundwork for Wakeman's future pioneering of new age music."

August 7th, 1973, Morgan Studios, London.

© Laurens Van Houten / Frank White Photo Agency

August 7th, 1973, Morgan Studios, London.

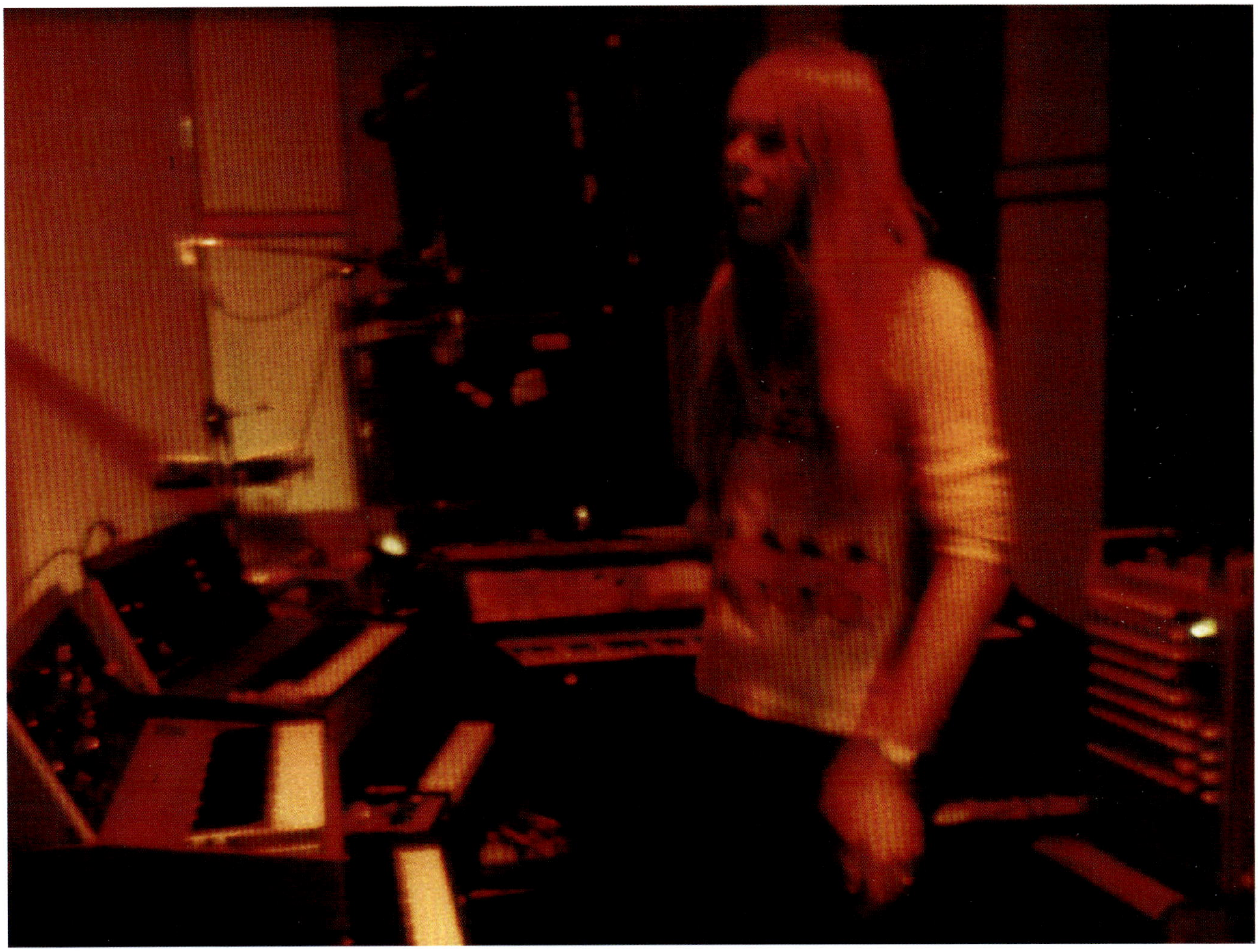

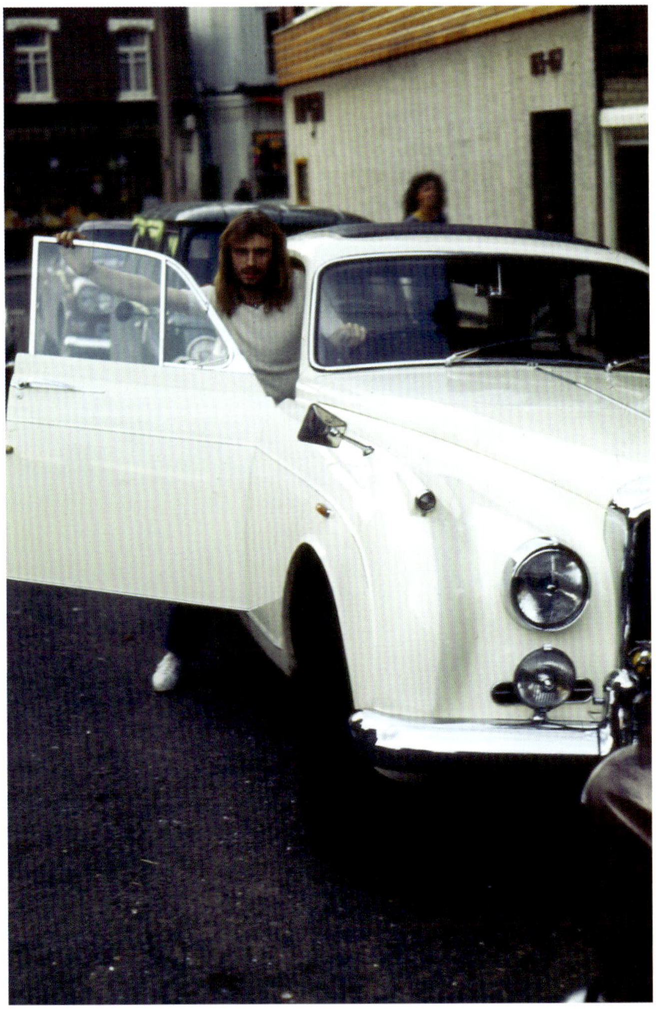

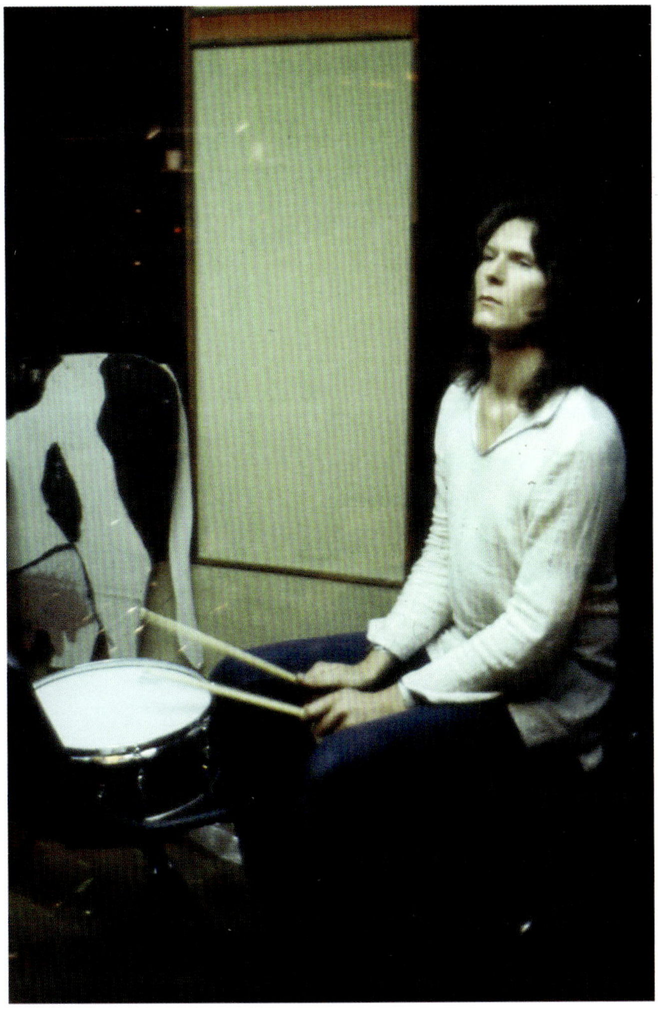

August 7th, 1973, Morgan Studios, London.

November 23rd, 1973, The Rainbow, London.

© Laurens Van Houten / Frank White Photo Agency

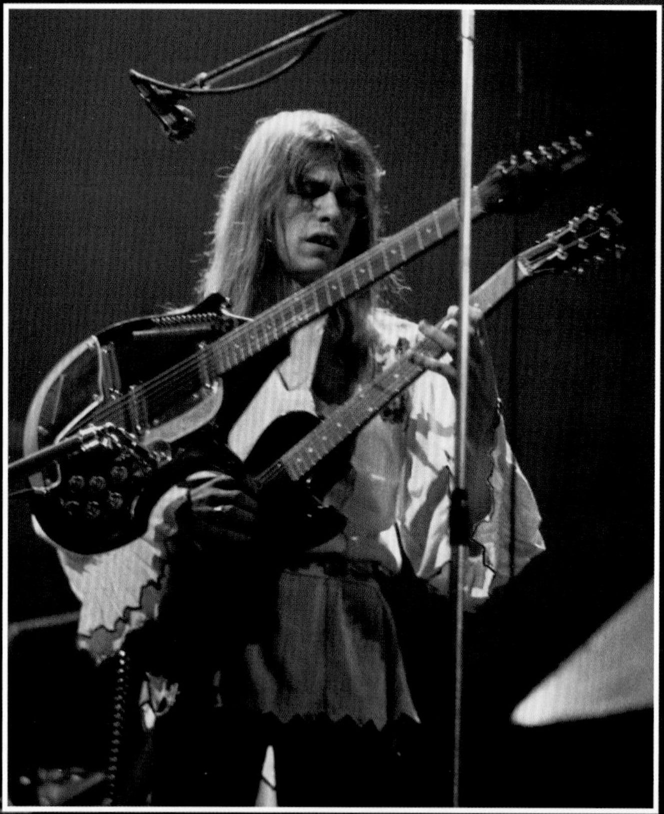

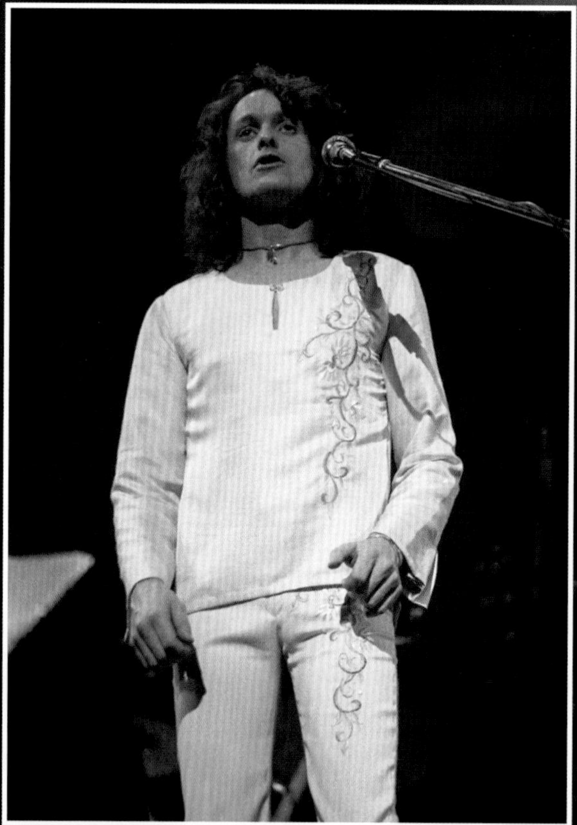

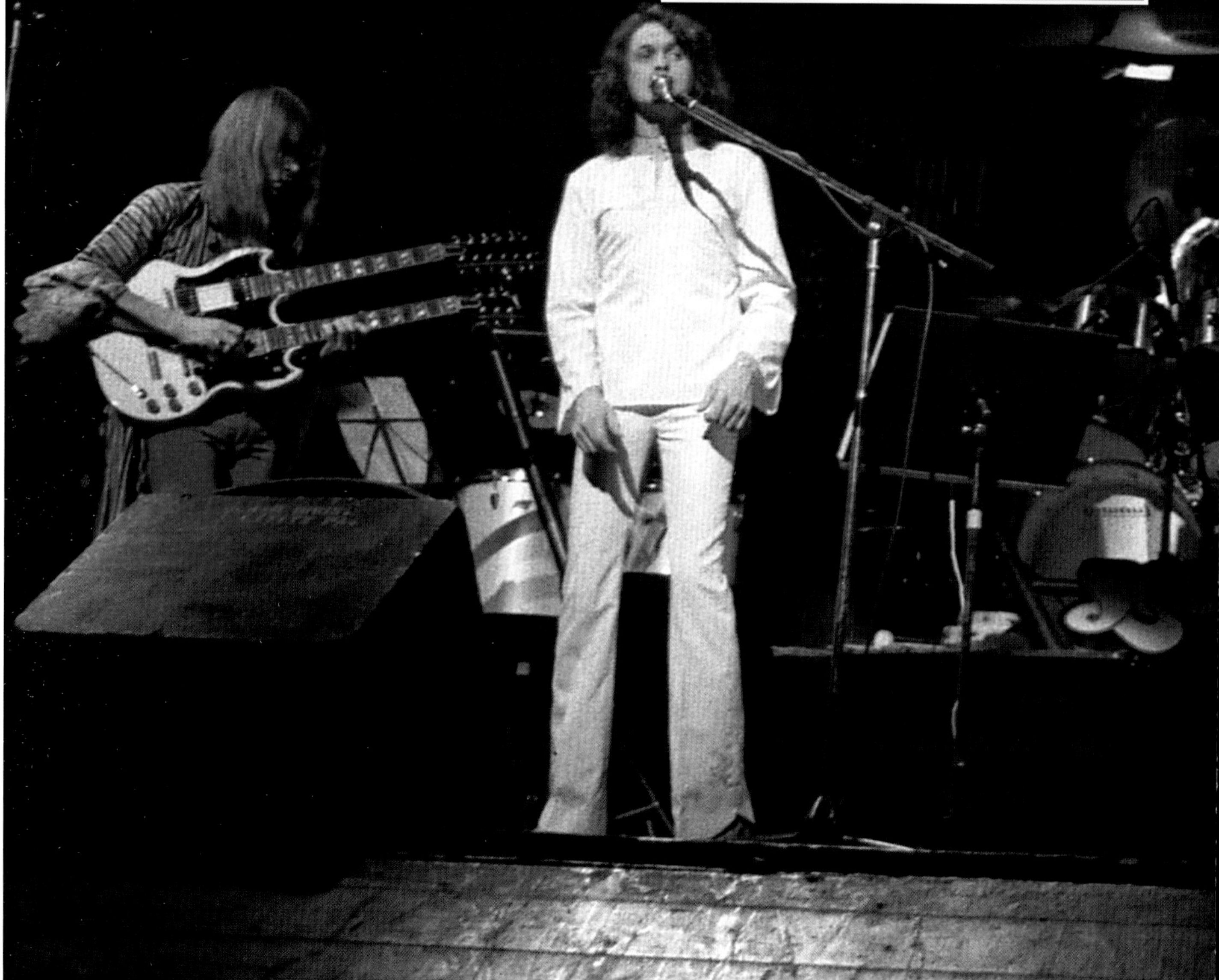

November 23rd, 1973,
The Rainbow, London.

© Laurens Van Houten / Frank White Photo Agency

November 23rd, 1973, The Rainbow, London.

© Laurens Van Houten / Frank White Photo Agency

96

© Laurens Van Houten / Frank White Photo Agency

97

**December 14, 1973.** Yes, issue, in the UK, their sixth studio album, a double LP concept package called *Tales from Topographic Oceans*. The album is produced by Eddie Offord, who has now done four studio albums for the band, as well as engineering on *Time and a Word*. The sprawling album, with one track on each of its four sides, is summarily ridiculed by critics and the industry, in large part due to its meandering music, but also its almost religious cult-like lyrical musings. Nonetheless, the record ships gold, rising to No.6 on the Billboard charts.

**Steve Howe:**
"Topographic *was our indulgence. Most people think of it as that, but it was a musical indulgence where we didn't see why we couldn't have more time than we had on the last record. And that's not really a failing. But yeah, we did that because we really did have space. We had the writing power, we had the arrangement power, to go beyond the size of* Close to the Edge. *But I don't think size is really it. I think it was just that we dreamed up this concept about the four sides, and had the music to fulfil it. And all we needed was the group's*

enthusiasm, which wasn't there all the time. Jon and I did have some uphill struggles with the other three guys in the band, who weren't always convinced we were doing the right thing. We somehow convinced them, for better or worse."

"And I guess Topographic is just our exuberant, over-the-top record that I guess you'd have to like Yes quite a lot to appreciate. But I'd like to point out one thing. When it came out, of course the press slagged it like mad. Rick left the band, virtually because all his friends said they hated it so much. And that was really dumb. I've got a review of Fragile from the Melody Maker which slagged Fragile totally. Not wishing to demean your trade, your business, but sometimes reviewers go too far. And, well, they tried to kill Fragile. It didn't work. They tried to kill Tales. It didn't work. Because a year later this record was being heralded by Yes fans as a masterpiece. I'm not saying it is a masterpiece, but it's certainly a lot of Yes music."

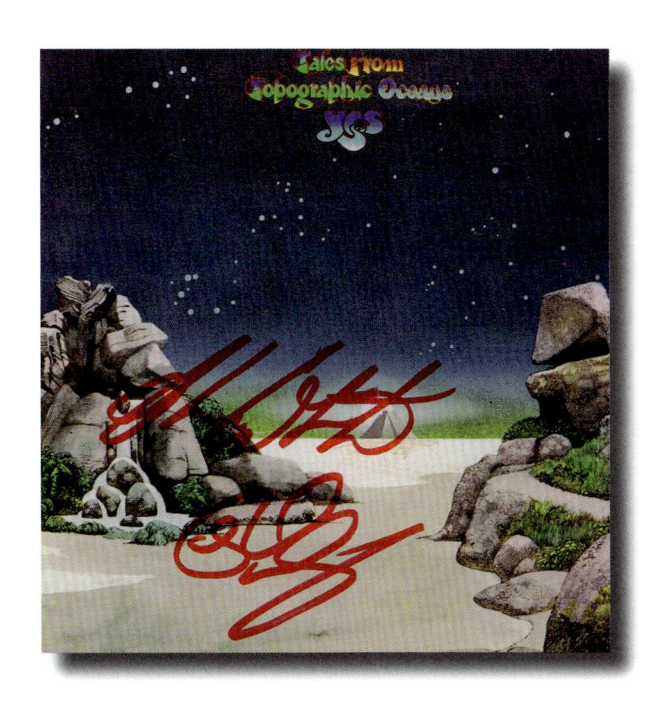

### Rick Wakeman:

"You see, what people sometimes forget, is that while I'm in the band, I'm a fan as well. You can be in the band and be a fan of the band as well. All the times I've not been in the band, I've been a fan of the band. And as a fan, I think I'm as entitled as anybody else to say I love that album, that's quite good or oh, I don't like that. And Topographic Oceans, there would have never been a problem with it if the CD had been around. The problem was, we had a little bit too much material for a single album, and we had not enough material for a double album."

"So you do one of two things. You either say, okay, we'll make a nice single album, or you expand. And we went down the expansion route, but we didn't have the material. So there was padding for days to get a track to each side. And a lot of the padding was junk. And I'll stand by that 'til this day. If the CD had been around, we would have had probably 50 minutes, maybe an hour. One of the tracks might have been ten, one of them might have been 20, one of them might have been 14. But they would have had their natural length, not, oh, let's bash away here and do something to make it longer. How long is that—14? Oh, we need another four minutes. Bash away a bit longer. There was too much padding, and I know where the padding is and it pains me every time I hear it."

"But it was back in those days when, you go back into the '70s, and everything was black and white. So I said what I thought, and when I said something was very black, others said it was very white. Back then we weren't in a mature situation where we could sit and say, hold on a minute, let's talk about this. So to me it was black and white; I hated it. But the truth, *music is just too languished and insufferably relentless in its somewhat trashy advance unto resolution. But after a heavy-ish cornucopic miasma of fast music, resolution most certainly arrives, in the closing percussive jam, where each member had been given a drummer's toy to bash (Sepultura does it better!). After this, Jon sings a mildly moving bit of love balladeering, a moment that is as personable as parts of side one, and then after a bit more jiggling and doodling, it's all over."*

*"Quite the baffling bunch of sonics by any measure, Tales is nevertheless a necessary record to the Yes saga, the point to which the band had to go so they could snap back on track, to represent contrast against their more urgent material, essentially to provide lush jungle terrain for the fan who has grown tired of the manicured lawns—or at least semi-managed parklands—of the more accessible and popular Yes records."*

# Tales From Topographic Oceans

## Yes

Available on Atlantic Records and Tapes K80001 Cassette K480001 Cartridge K880001

"*Relayer* was almost as hard as *Topographic*, even though it was only a single album. It was a tough album to make. It was, once again, conceptualised to the nth degree. Patrick Moraz joined us, and we had to kind of contain him as well as push him and let him lead occasionally. We had to contain him because in a way, that wheel on the Minimoog, the wheel on that synth, was one of the sounds he liked most. And we didn't want him to touch the wheel and make that vibrato. So in the way the guitar wasn't playing blues and therefore wasn't playing vibrato, we also didn't want the group to suddenly sound like, you know, Chick Corea and Return to Forever. We didn't really want it to sound extremely jazzy or extremely fusion, because we wanted to keep our identity. So one of the charming things was keeping Patrick under control. He had a lot of breadth to his writing, but sometimes he said he wanted to get more jazzy. And we kind of went, 'Hmmm, yeah, eh;' we didn't always agree. So in a way, *Topographic* and *Relayer* were as experimental as *Close to the Edge*. More so, in a way, because at least *Close to the Edge* had more of a stable lineup."
**Steve Howe**

# 1974 to 1976: Relayer

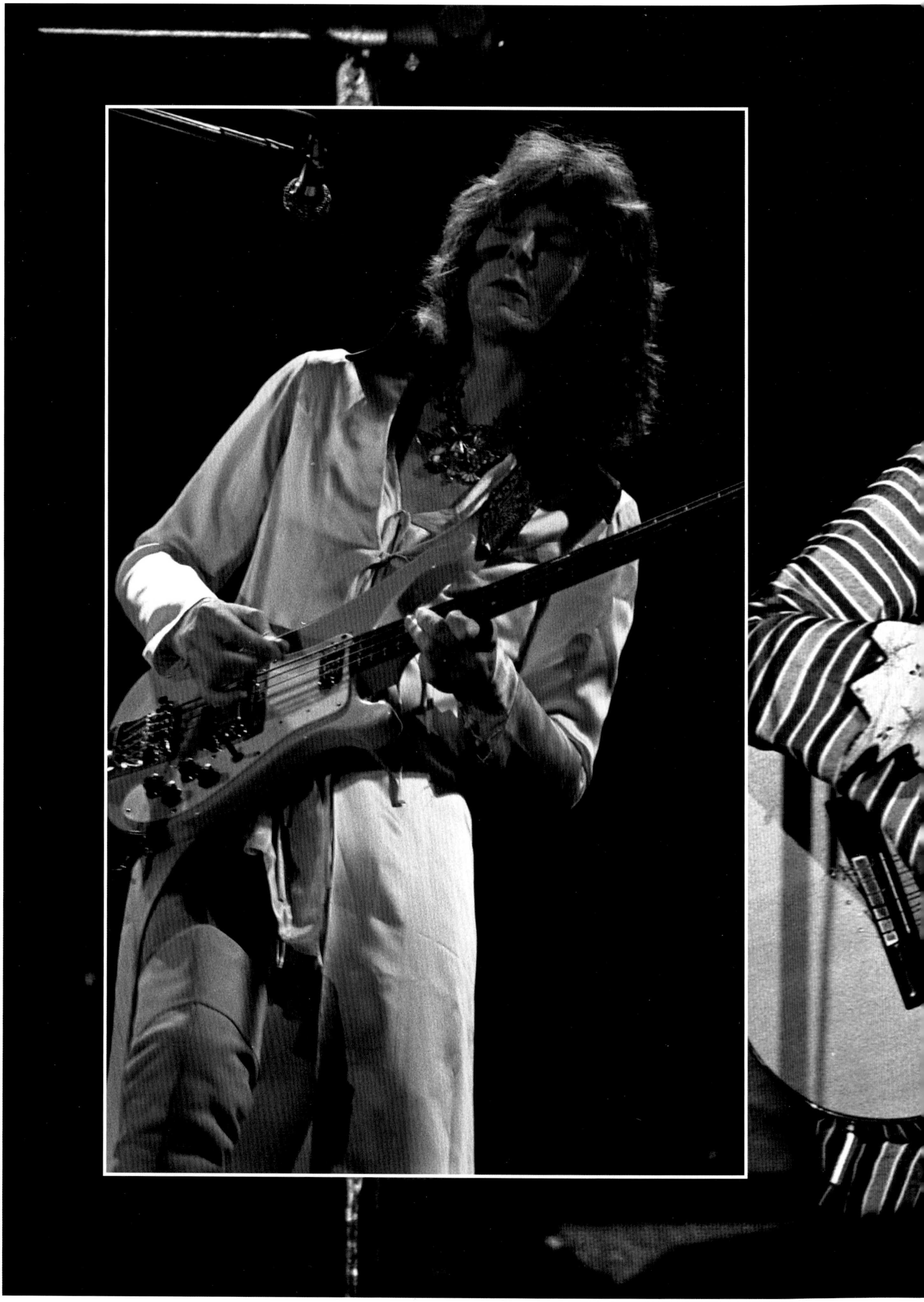

April 17th, 1974, Ahoy, Rotterdam, Netherlands.

© Laurens Van Houten / Frank White Photo Agency

April 17th, 1974, Ahoy, Rotterdam, Netherlands.

April 17th, 1974, Steve Howe at the Ahoy, Rotterdam, Netherlands.

Jon Anderson reading a Dutch paper in Amsterdam, April 1974.

**February 18, 20, 1974.** Yes play two shows at Madison Square Gardens, sponsored by *Melody Maker* magazine. The sold-out shows gross about $260,000, the reporting of which got the magazine in a bit of hot water.

**May 9, 1974.** Rick Wakeman issues his second solo album, *Journey to the Centre of the Earth*, which, like the debut, certifies gold in the US. The concept album also goes gold in the UK and Canada and garners a Grammy nomination.

### Rick Wakeman, in 1974:

"I first read the book when I was nine, would you believe it, and I never understood it. Then I read it again when I went to grammar school; we had to do it as part of a syllabus thing. I thought it was an amazing book then. Funnily enough, I read it yet again just after I got married about four years ago and I thought it would be a fantastic thing to put to music because it's such a commanding story. I did actually work out a format to do it before the Henry VIII thing. I thought rather than do a haphazard thing, I'd do Henry first which wasn't anything near such an expensive project and I'd then just save me shekels sort of thing and plan the gig in advance. We're just up to about £30,000 at the moment."

"(For a band) I deliberately chose people who weren't known because the concert had to stand up on its own by the music. Take Tommy: some of the orchestrations in it were really fantastic but totally lost because the whole stage was full up with faces that came on to thunderous applause and it was more an event than a piece of music. There are some bloody fine musicians about which nobody has ever heard of."

### Author review:

"Ol' Rick, the svengali of super serious silliness is at it again, going well beyond the call of duty, constructing an elaborate concept record complete with symphony, narration and lots of acid-placid pictures. This one's based on the Jules Verne story, Wakeman concentrating on a scant few themes, a) the beginning of the journey from Germany to Iceland; b) a little metaphysical

Jon Anderson practising his air guitar in Amsterdam, April 1974.

Chris Squire, signed photo 1974.

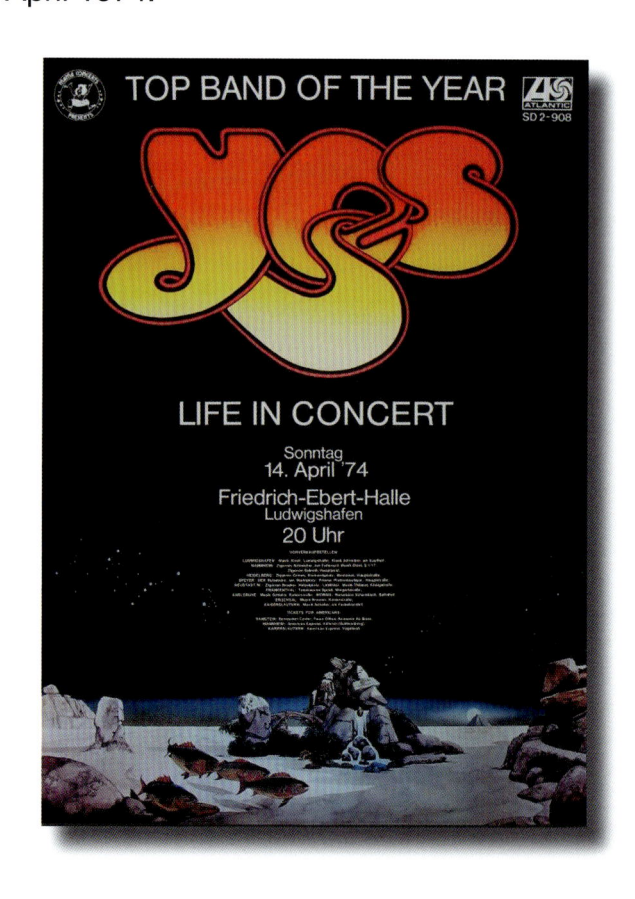

*recollection of a life gone by; c) a bizarre battle between two sea monsters (the included eight-page booklet shows them atop a couple of frosty pints!); and d) a depiction of the destination, or forest, which the included photos would have us believe looks like the inside of a mouth."*

*"Musically, it's all a little much (like that fall-down-laughing Deep Purple thing), a classical record with rock passages and lots of Wakeman synthesizer worming around the place. There's very few lyrics, but the narration fills in the gaps. That is if you care, Wakeman breaking all the rules of restraint, leap-frogging prog into the Spinal Tap zone, proving himself the ultimate puffy, puffed-up emperor of boffo. But hey, the goofy music fan of the day liked it, propelling the record to No.1 on the UK charts, and aiding in Rick's decision to leave Yes after an unpleasant sail on* Topographic Oceans."

**May 18, 1974.** Rick, on the phone from his home in Devon, tells Brian Lane that he is indeed quitting the band, confirmed in his decision by the material he was hearing coming out of the *Relayer* sessions. Moments later he gets a call from A&M's Terry O'Neil telling him that his new solo album had just hit No.1 on the British charts.

### Rick Wakeman on his saddest times touring with Yes:
"Tales from Topographic Oceans tour. It's very hard to play music that you are not into. You can play the notes, but there is so much more to music than playing notes."

**July 1974.** Rick is admitted to hospital after a minor heart attack.

**August 1974.** After auditioning Greek synthesizer magician Vangelis Papathanassiou for a couple of weeks, the band put through the paces Patrick Moraz, from post-Nice band Refugee, who plays for the guys in Chris Squire's barn, using Vangelis' keyboards—he gets the gig.

### Vangelis Papathanassiou on quashing the idea of joining Yes:
"To me, there are only two types of music—honest music and dishonest music. Now, when I listen to Yes' music, I am conscious of the fact that it is Occidental music. It is very English in its nature. Now I am not like that. I'm not saying I'm an Oriental, but Greece has such a rich heritage and there are certain similarities between some ethnic Greek music and Chinese music. It would be very difficult for me to play with any band. I wouldn't like to have my music limited by the abilities of one particular group of people."

### Patrick Moraz on his audition:
"I remember it very well. It was a Wednesday afternoon, and what I saw was incredible. There was a trailer lined up with vegetarian food, an army of roadies, amazing monitor systems. I mean, Refugee was selling out 3000-seat halls in England, but this was a whole new plateau. We introduced each other, had some tea, and then they played what was to become 'Sound Chaser' on Relayer— just the middle part, because I would write the introduction later. I was totally overwhelmed, because they played so fast and so precisely and so well."

**August 1974.** Canadian hard rockers Bachman-Turner Overdrive issue their third album, *Not Fragile*.

### Randy Bachman:
"'Not Fragile' is a great track because Fred Turner wrote that and it was the antithesis of the Yes album, which is called Fragile, which was such intricate playing. I'm not putting down Yes, because I really like them and their sound; they had some good hits. But the Fragile album is like the ultimate, you know, almost being too much, almost too cluttered. Obviously this was before the heavy metal speed guys, but there was a lot of stuff to ingest in your brain when all

*you wanted to do is enjoy the music. So Fred came up with this absolutely simple, mindless but headbanging riff (sings it), to scream and sing over. And the thing about that was that anybody can pick up the guitar and play 'Not Fragile.' Nobody could go play the* Fragile *album by Yes; that was the difference. One was the LCD, the lowest common denominator that always ran through the band. That's what BTO was, the lowest common denominator. You don't want the guy who's 40, who's been studying guitar for 30 years, to buy your record, to learn your riff. You want the 13-year-old kid who can't play, to buy your record to learn your riff, and you want him to be able to learn and play the riff because then he'll keep playing your records and keep buying them. I learned that long ago."*

**August – October 1974.** The band work on what will become *Relayer*, at New Pipers, Chris Squire's home in Virginia Water, Surrey, using Eddie Offord's mobile equipment, with mixing to take place at Advision.

*Patrick Moraz, on whether he joined Yes through band contact or management contact:*
"Both, personal contact with Jon Anderson which had been arranged by my very good friend Ray Gomez, guitarist extraordinaire, also by Chris Welch, the main journalist for the music paper Melody Maker and also through a request by Brian Lane, Yes' manager at that time. Then through the request by the whole group. Apparently, it was a unanimous decision and the invitation came quite instantly. The day after I played with them for the very first time, I got a call telling me I was in the band as an equal member, and my presence was being requested immediately! Personally, I wasn't sure I wanted to get into Yes at the time because I was doing film scores—I was working on two movies at the same time, one with my friend Gerard Depardieu—and I was still under professional commitment with Refugee. Although we were on the verge of splitting up Refugee, we still had some concerts to do, promoting our first and only album Refugee, which had entered at No.28 in the Melody Maker British music charts a few weeks earlier and was still climbing."

*Steve Howe:*
"Relayer—and this is almost the same for Topographic—it's a very stylistically definitive record. Because we invented it right there and then. We worked out how to make 20-minute tracks that we took three days to record. We wouldn't stay in there for three days, but when we came back the next day, we carried on with the song. It was a quest, it was a mission, it was a concept."

**October 6, 1974.** King Crimson issue their seminal *Red* album, simultaneous with Robert Fripp announcing that the band was breaking up. Bill Bruford is fine with it, up for whatever comes next.

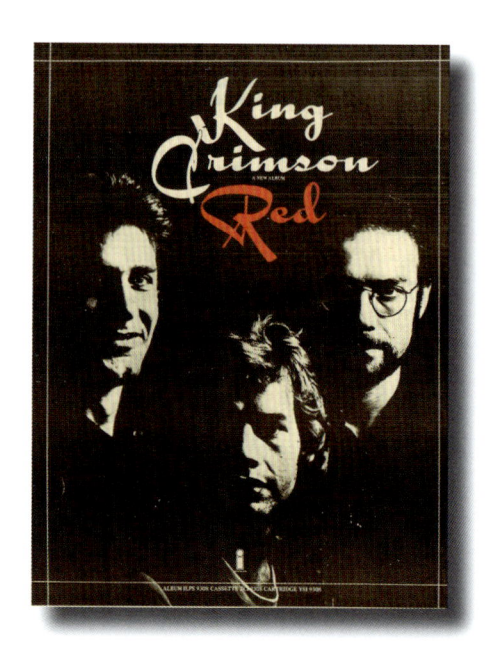

**November 18, 1974.** Yes rivals Genesis issue a conceptual double album answer to *Topographic Oceans*, called *The Lamb Lies Down on Broadway*. Unlike the Yes record, however, history views *Lamb* as a classic, maybe the band's greatest triumph, and indeed the record most cited as a rival to *Close to the Edge* as the greatest prog rock album of all time.

**November 28, 1974.** Yes issue, in the UK, their seventh studio album, *Relayer*. It is a dense, jazzy, opaque album for the band, but not as inscrutable as its preposterous predecessor, *Tales from Topographic Oceans*. The record peaks at No.4 in the UK and No.5 in the US, despite its challenges. As well, the album goes gold in the US within a month, which speaks favourably to the record buying public's willingness to support complicated progressive rock. Roger Dean offers one of his most monochromatic covers, the idea inspired by Tolkien, with the scene representing a potential Garden of Eden, hence the presence of the snake.

### Patrick Moraz:

"When we started to record Relayer, some of the music had already been written and rehearsed by Chris, Jon, Steve and Alan. I contributed as much as I could to the overall picture of the pieces. However, it is a fact that Steve used quite a lot of tracks for his many overdubs everywhere on the album, except when there is no guitar at all, which is a rare occasion. We all participated in the compositions and the final arrangements, even if most of the 'songs' were originally composed somewhat more by Jon, and Steve in some instances. I liked to work with Jon and Chris, especially. Alan was always contributing some very good rhythmic ideas. I also worked quite a lot with Steve during the whole time I was in Yes."

### Rick Wakeman:

"Relayer is a funny thing. When I left after Topographic Oceans, I just couldn't get it musically. I thought, you've got to give and take. No point in being part of something you can't give to. When I heard Relayer—I was actually asked to review it for the BBC—I said look, if I say I like it, you'll say that's because they're your friends. And if I say I don't like it, then you'll say, well that's because you're not there anymore. And I played it, and I didn't like it. But I was *really pleased that I didn't like it. It was far too jazzy and freeform, which I didn't like. And I said it's not my cup of tea, but I'm really pleased that it sounds like this. And the guy scratched his head and said why? And I said, well, if I had heard something that was melodic, that was full of Yes thematic things and melody, I would be really pissed-off. Because, I said, I left the band, because I felt it was heading this route. And in hearing this album, I said, there isn't anything I could have offered to this album, absolutely nothing I could offer to any one of these pieces at all. So I said I'm really pleased. I'm pleased I made the right decision to leave the band when I did."*

### Jon Anderson on "The Gates of Delirium," which encompasses all of side one of Relayer:

"I actually wrote that on the piano and then brought it to the band. I had this crazy idea and just gave it to them and they understood me. That's why I worked on Yes' music. I didn't want to be a pop star; I wanted to make some great music, and I think we have over the last 40 years."

### Alan White:

"There are a lot of periods where Chris and myself had a very adventurous time in the studio, let's put it that way. Topographic Oceans had a lot of very strange percussive and bass work on it, but Relayer was also very inventive, with songs like 'Sound Chaser' and 'The Gates of Delirium.' Basically it was because we were constructing music as a five-piece. Pieces weren't constructed before we entered the situation, so some of the music was structured around the rhythm section."

**November 8, 1974 – August 23, 1975.** Yes fulfil the dates of their *Relayer* tour, with Gryphon supporting on the front half and Ace picking up in mid-May. Over Moraz's time with the band, his live rig would expand from five keyboards in 1974, to 14 in 1975 and in his final year, 24 instruments necessarily arranged on two levels.

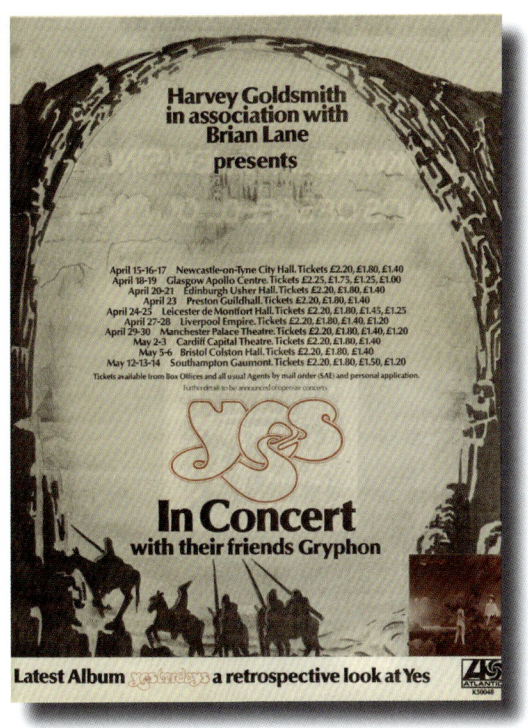

### Steve Howe on "To Be Over" and Relayer:
*"I have voted that one as one of my favourite tracks and Relayer as one of my favourite albums. The sleeve is one of my favourite sleeves. It was a very combustibles time. We had already achieved our first major big stepping stone. We got to play the 20-minute style piece and we were in this enormous landscape where we could do things like that. We did Topographic. We had not even absorbed all of the criticism from when we changed keyboard players and we still went in and did another 20-minute piece. We did an album almost identical to* Close to the Edge *in structure. I think it's a really exciting format for Yes."*

### Journalist Ed Sciaky:
*"Relayer is reassuring. The production, by Yes and near-member Eddie Offord, is flawless and astounding. The role of Moraz' keyboards is naturally subdued from Wakeman's, but so is that of Jon Anderson's essential vocals. The resulting greater individual importance of Steve Howe's brilliant guitar work, Chris Squire's foreground bass lines and Alan White's powerful drumming, leads to the most unified blend of musicians Yes has yet produced, playing music that's melodic, cohesive and concise. Relayer is exactly the album Yes needed to survive the crises, convince sceptics, and at the same time, further the enchantment of believers."*

### Cash Box, on Relayer:
*"When you're dealing with genius you always find some startling new twists to what your preconceived notions are. In the case of Yes' new LP, there are but three cuts and only one record. But there's a wealth of musical dexterity, innovation and continual professionalism. The quintet is into violent mood changes here with elaborate instrumental passages leading up to the telling lyric lines. Listen and you'll find wonder and amazement here."*

### Jon Anderson, speaking in 1975:
*"In general, there's no way you can get to the truth about life through drugs or magic, things like that. It's within you. It's there, it's resting, and you can bring it to life any time you want."*

November 20th, 1974, Madison Square Garden, New York.

© John T. Comerford III / Frank White Photo Agency

**1975.** Trevor Rabin issues his first album, *Boys Will Be Boys*, with his band Rabbitt. The record would be moderately distributed in North America, more so than 1976's *A Croak and a Grunt in the Night*.

*Trevor Rabin, on moving to the US because of A&R guru John Kalodner:*
"He is one of the best A&R people that I've ever met, even though, at the end of the day, he dropped me. There is nobody like him in the business anymore; he is a true genius. Rabbit had saturated the South African market and we needed to try to break elsewhere. Management had a very different way of thinking on how we should do that and it really screwed it up. It led to me leaving. I am happy to say that the guys in Rabbitt are still close."

**January 8, 1975.** A portion of "The Gates of Delirium" called "Soon" is issued as a UK single from *Relayer*, backed with "Sound Chaser."

*Jon Anderson on "Soon:"*
"It's a very difficult song that you're singing to God and saying, 'Come over here. What's happened? You know we want some light.' We're asking the Divine to show some light in this world, as we need a reason to be here. And, of course, over the years I have more light every day. I think we all have the same spirituality deep inside and we grow to learn more about it all the time, and we try very hard to become better people as we grow. We search all the time for the truth. We learn more about the world and we can't have thoughts like, 'We are better than them' or 'They are not good enough for God.' This is a very bad way of thinking, you know?"

*Steve Howe on the band's predilection for epic-length composition:*
"That is one of the things that I am most proud of with Yes. In the mid-'70s we used to say that we were purposely un-commercial. Atlantic really did want us to have hits. We had 'Roundabout' which was a very deserving kind of hit because it so encapsulated the style of Yes. We just haven't written enough songs like that but we should. It gave us a foot in the door with Atlantic. On Close to the Edge they asked, 'What's the single?' but we really didn't have one. They were quite happy that we sold millions of albums so they were not ready to kick us out the door! There was a marvellous leverage for originality and lack of commerciality. We had people in America that were playing this on the radio. We were one of the only bands to do that. That was based on our reputation."

*Alan White:*
"*Relayer* was a totally experimental period as far as playing drums go. Not that Topographic wasn't; *Topographic* had a lot of intricate bass and drums, with the rhythm section being adventurous in trying to find new rhythms, with a lot of direction and ethnic music in the background. Relayer was an extension of that, but obviously down the road a bit, after we'd been playing that for a while. I find songs like 'Sound Chaser' very exciting. Nobody was doing anything quite like that at the time, where songs sped up and slowed down three or four times within the course of a song, that kind of experimentation. And I remember recording some of the percussion on 'Gates of Delirium;' Jon Anderson and myself used to stop in at a scrap yard every day and pick up pieces of car, and we made a kind of framework of pieces of cars in the studio that we could bang on (laughs). We'd go through the car scrap yard, and find springs and pieces of metal. So some of the percussion on that is actually us playing pieces of cars in the studio, making big clanking noises."

**February – September 1975.** Chris Squire works on material for his first solo album at Virginia Water, Surrey Sound Studios and Morgan Studios. Yes alumni Bill Bruford and Patrick Moraz contribute to the sessions.

### Chris Squire, on his influences:

"Different people have different ideas: people compare me to Jimi Hendrix in some ways. I used to like Jimi Hendrix's bass playing very much (laughing) so I'm sure I borrowed some ideas of his for the bass. But then again, I had many great influences in my career, like Paul McCartney and Bill Wyman and, of course, the late great John Entwistle and Jack Bruce—all these people have been great influences on me. And of course, all the members of Yes that have been coming and leaving and coming back: I've learnt from all those musicians a lot too, from their influences onto Yes which has given Yes maybe a different look every time we changed somebody. So that's been a big learning curve for me."

**February 28, 1975.** Yes issue a compilation of songs mostly from their first two albums, called *Yesterdays*. The album reaches No.27 in the UK and No.17 in the US.

### Jon Anderson, in 1977:

"We try to do something that involves intricate themes which won't be forgotten. We have a pattern but at the same time we like to surprise people by developing and expanding on logics. We haven't compromised with record companies, we haven't let them dictate to us and we haven't lost many of our original ethics. The only compromise we did was to release Yesterdays, a retrospective look at what we'd been doing. We've never wanted to produce three-minute dance tunes. In my songs I've always tried to use ideas that affect people. Listening to Yes, I hope people will be able to discover things about themselves. I hope they'll be as inspired as I am when I listen to classical music. You can think deeply and realize the music is bringing out your own thoughts."

**March 12, 1975.** Atlantic Records announces that the *Yessongs* "feature-length motion picture" will launch in quadraphonic theatres in Madison, WI, Charlotte NC, and Cincinnati OH, to be followed by showings in 20 other US cities.

**April 1975.** Rick Wakeman continues his streak, landing his third RIAA-certified gold album in a row with *The Myths and Legends of King Arthur and the Knights of the Round Table*.

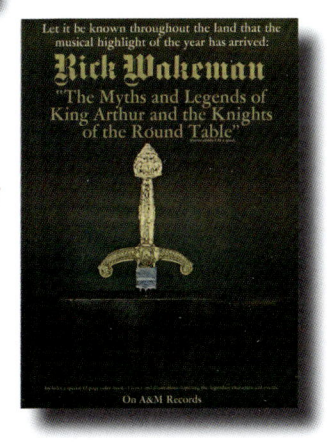

127

***Rick Wakeman on experiencing heart attacks, plus the making of King Arthur:***
"Three actually and the third was not very minor! I wrote the album while in hospital. It's a parallel musical autobiography. I was told I would not be able to play live again and should retire. There is much of me in that album, personally. The main theme is probably the best I have managed to produce."

**May 23 – 25, 1975.** Alan White records the material for what will be his first solo album.

**May 30, 31, June 1, 1975.** Rick Wakeman's latest concept album, *The Myths and Legends of King Arthur and the Knights of the Round Table*, is presented as a skating pageant, at Wembley Empire Pool.

***Uncredited writer for New Musical Express, April 5, 1975:***
"It is planned as a colourful spectacle, involving lavish costumes and a huge castle setting, with the ice representing the moat. Seventeen skaters will be taking part and Wakeman will make his entrance on a white horse. Supporting Wakeman musically will be the 48-piece English Chamber Choir, the eight-piece Nottingham Festival Singers and his group, the English Rock Ensemble. Narrator, as on the album, is Royal Shakespeare Company actor Terry Taplin and the musical director is David Meacham. Another innovation will be the special "Sound in Around" system, which involves the PA being suspended from the roof."

**October 31, 1975.** Steve Howe issues his first solo album, *Beginnings*. Included on it is current Yes drummer Alan White and past drummer Bill Bruford, along with Patrick Moraz. The album reaches No.22 on the UK charts and No.65 in the US.

***Patrick Moraz:***
"In the very early part of 1975 already, we somehow had discussed the idea of doing—each and every one of us—a solo album. Steve asked me if I wanted to take part in his own Beginnings album. I said, 'Sure I would love to!' Then he gave me a tape with a few notes on it and asked me if I could arrange and orchestrate it like Vivaldi. I said I would do my best and I worked on it for about three weeks. When I came to play him the demo and show him all the work I had done with the piece, 'Beginnings,' he loved it immediately and he told me that we would record it. And we did. I also played the harpsichord on some other tunes with him on the album. I also conducted the chamber orchestra for the recording sessions. Of course, my arrangement sounded nothing like Vivaldi, but it had its own personality and uniqueness to it."

"Steve—I remember the moment very well—was kind of in shock and at the same time very happily surprised that I had come up with the whole arrangement like that and wanted to use it immediately, without any changes. We recorded the whole session with Steve, on acoustic guitar. Along with my final harpsichord parts, I conducted the orchestra, while he eventually re-recorded his guitar parts at a later date. The video was taped also at a later date."

***Steve Howe:***
"Patrick Moraz went on to play some remarkable things on my album, Beginnings. He really surprised me when I heard 'Will o' the Wisp' and other songs that he played on. And then to the second album, there's the amazing Mellotron and keyboard work and piano work he did on 'All's a Chord'—really remarkable."

*Author review:*

"Steve Howe's first solo record is wonderfully predictable, Steve proving his inherent, comfortable Yes-ness with an airy, idealistic, dreamy display of hippie music that surely any Yes fan could appreciate. The overall sound is benevolent and homey, close, countrified and folksy, Steve playing most guitar and bass and singing every track in his somewhat fragile but warm style. It's a voice that is not without eccentricity and flat notes, but the minstrel-like DIY good intention of it all erases any thoughts of critical malice."

"Most tracks mix effortlessly many acoustic and electric guitar textures, with side one closer 'Lost Symphony' adding an arresting horn pattern to what is the bravest, most ambitious and perhaps lasting track on the record. Side two opener 'Beginnings' features Steve treading ethereal footsteps through an eight-piece orchestra, whereas 'Ram' tender-picks to completing trilogy status with 'The Clap' and 'Mood for a Day' as a light-hearted Dixie rag extraordinaire."

"Many of the other tracks are quite busy, falling just this side of prog, more like complicated folk rock, Steve making good use of Alan White's blocky exuberance, and to a lesser extent, the sticks of David Oberle and Bill Bruford, whose two tracks are fairly straight-forward, even if closer 'Break Away from It All' is the rockiest thing on the record."

"Still, one listens to this record not for progressive brilliance, but for Howe's particular idealism, bolstered by his fluid if edgy, very painterly guitar tones. Eddie Offord's homespun recording values also help the cause, the seasoned sonic sculptor of Yes providing grounded and objective separation between instruments, and an overall home-baked humanity to the project. As with the best of Yes, Beginnings takes the discerning listener to meadows of contemplation, any bluster more than doubly paid off by soothing warm melodies, and a timeless lyrical invitation to relax."

**November 7, 1975.** Chris Squire issues his first solo album, in the UK, called *Fish Out of Water*, with US release to follow December 30th. The album reaches No.25 on the UK charts and No.69 in the US. Fish is Chris' nickname, derived from the fact that the notorious slow-moving Squire spends a long time in the bathtub and in the shower, which was a particular irritant back when Yes had their own communal band house at 50A Munster Road, Fulham, in which all the band and their girlfriends lived, save for Tony Kaye who lived in neighbouring Chelsea.

*Chris Squire:*

"I enjoyed doing that album. At the time I was working with Andrew Jackman, who'd been a friend of mine since I was a teenager. And he was a great arranger and even helped co-write some of the material. Unfortunately, he's no longer with us. So that was a fantastic experience, that whole orchestral molding of that album and the ideas that we put into it. And his brother, Gregory, was the engineer on it, and in fact Greg Jackman is still around these days making hits. Very exciting time; it was made in my first home studio in my house in England. So there were a lot of good vibes around that album. Hopefully soon, I'm going to be doing some live shows with Steve Hackett, because we have a project together that will emerge in the near future, and when we go out and do that live, I hope to do some of Fish Out of Water, which will really be the first time that it's been done properly."

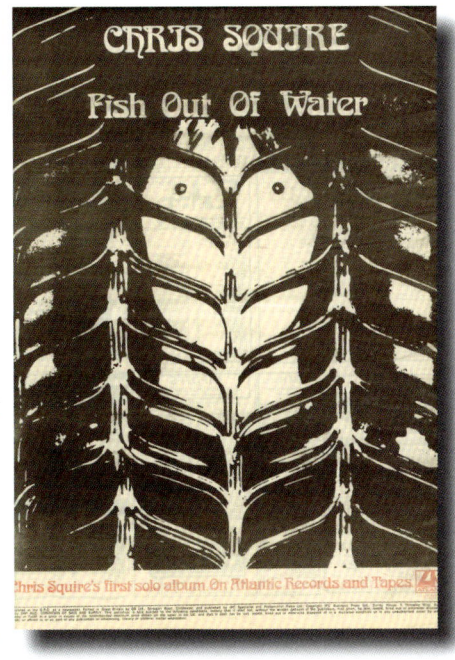

**1976.** John Wetton, Rick Wakeman and Bill Bruford float the idea of forming a band called British Bulldog.

**1976.** Harvest Records reissue Tomorrow's one and only record, from 1968. *Tomorrow* was guitarist Steve Howe's first album.

**February 1976.** Illinois' Starcastle issue their self-titled debut, on Epic. The band would crank out four records through 1978. Their claim to fame? An astonishing recreation of Yes' classic sound, with Starcastle attempting and achieving such an accurate and bald-faced tribute to Yes, that not even any of the myriad neo-neo-prog bands of the 1990s would ever dare try compete.

*Rick Wakeman:*
"I haven't heard them. If they're good musicians, perhaps they'll develop a style of their own. Everybody plays other people's music when they start. I remember Keith pinched half of Jimmy Smith's licks for some Nice records."

**March 1976.** Alan White issues his first solo album, *Ramshackled*, with members of the Alan Price Set. The album fails to chart in the US, but reaches No.41 in the UK.

*Author review:*
"Alan White lets fly with perhaps the most churlish, eccentric and blender-made of the batched solo records clustered in and around 1976. I mean, not like he does much here, writing nothing, and letting one of his earlier, non-recording bands define the record, White doing... well, who knows what? In any event, 'his' record is a cyclone of weird musics, not so much prog, just off-kilter, similar soul tones to Peter Hammill, Steve Hillage and Ian Anderson colliding with American over-profusions like Chicago, Santana, Steely Dan and even Zappa."

"So this warm, likeable and unrestrained mish-mash of musical elements becomes a healthy, super-dated curio shop, not really all about drums, but about everybody packed into a VW bus. Reminds me of the spirit behind Ian Gillan Band, Gillan Glover, Ian Gillan, and for that matter Roger Glover's Mask, namely a yearning to be free of definition. So there's a baked dozen energy levels here, from the Jimbo mojo Zappa of 'Everybody' to the orchestrated hippie wash of 'Darkness,' brass everywhere in a '60s sort of Herb Alpert manner."

"Indeed, all sorts of '60s sounds bong through this record, 'Ooooh Baby' combining Tom Jones with Richie Havens, 'Giddy' doing a sort of CSNY thing. But the whole pop, fruity, brass-adelic hippie chumble becomes a total lark given that White's stamp is near non-existent, indeed the myriad of percussion flavours resulting in no central persona whatsoever. Closes with a nice Yes-type all-is-well-in-Eden number called 'Spring-Song of Innocence,' lead vocals by Jon Anderson, slippery axe work by Steve Howe. Original vinyl featured fancy embossed album cover (undermined by casual graphics), including an inner sleeve with pictures and painting and colourful felt pen lyrics on separate sheet. A cornball oddball to be sure."

**April 1976.** Alan White's solo album coughs up a UK-only single, in "Oooh! Baby (Go to Pieces)"/"One Way Rag."

**April 1, 1976.** Rush issue their landmark fourth album *2112*, which eventually sells triple platinum. Like Yes, Canada's famed prog rockers are known for long-form pieces but not particularly full concept albums. *2112* fits this description, being one side concept, one side not. The band is greatly influenced by Yes, in particular Geddy Lee, who cites Chris Squire as a huge inspiration.

**May 28 – August 23, 1976.** Yes embark on the *1976 Solo Albums Tour*, on which a small amount of solo material from the somewhat concurrent spate of solo albums from the guys is massaged into the set. Support for the front half comes from Pousette-Dart Band. New prog proposition Gentle Giant support in July.

*Jon Anderson, in 1977, on the side-trip into solo albums:*
"By the time we got into Relayer, there was a lot of feeling in the band that there are only certain kinds of music that you can play and still keep in touch with the audience. If you start to get too engrossed in your endeavour, it can be very dangerous if the fans of the band don't get off on it. The album suffered a bit in production, but it was a marvellous piece of music to play, and it went down very well with the live audience. It was a very gray cover, and we had a very gray feeling about it. Who's to know why? It made us think, 'Is this the right way for Yes to go? Do we want to get more involved?'"

"The idea of us all working on our solo albums was a very simple one—we weren't charged with emotion for Yes, but we were charged with emotion for ourselves. We didn't go away from each other, we just happened to be physically away from each other. It was good to get it out of our systems. And we knew that we were going to carry on with Yes; that was the most important point. (The industry) didn't look lightly on the solo projects. We didn't have any 'product,' as the business says, for two years, forgetting that we all made music. Whether it was good or bad is only relative to the people who enjoy it, or don't enjoy it. You can't always do what everybody wants. A lot of people enjoyed our solo works. When we came back together, it didn't hit us right away, but we all knew that Yes, in some ways, hopefully had to go further in reaching out to more people in order to survive."

**June 1976.** Patrick Moraz, as part of the plan for each of the members of the band to construct and issue a solo album, releases *I* or *i*, popularly known as *The Story of I*.

*Patrick Moraz:*
"The Story of I is an allegory about life and beyond. It takes place in an environment which implies the notion of virtuality. However, if the games are artificially monitored and use technologies which go beyond what is understood nowadays as digital and virtual, the emotions are very real, and the feelings are definitely human. The inspiration for The Story of I came to me during the course of an elevator ride in a newly-built hotel in America. The idea implanted itself in a flash. It immediately became clear that it was an allegory about life itself. What came to me was a way to present an abstract and spiritual train of thought under the guise of a concrete story, a kind of sci-fi story with plenty of symbolic narratives and figurative twists, with its own rites, games and rules as well as endless interactive situations. Always with a hopeful goal, however, with eternal light in sight, a sort of modern times search for the ever-elusive Holy Grail."

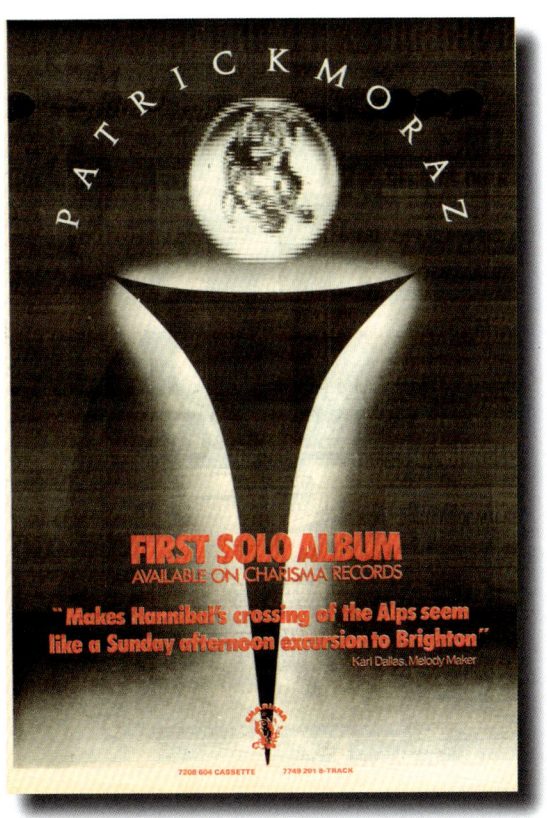

"For a first 'concept' album, the task was formidable and proved even more so as time passed. However, as the original idea was firmly rooted, the development of the whole work grew virtually at an exponential rate. All the elements came into place at the right time, even if over a period of a few months. I should have said 'almost at the right time.' A few timing problems and conflicting schedules presented themselves towards the end of the recording

"Jon Anderson was responsible for a lot of those lyrics. I'm not going to say that a lot of them didn't mean very much, because Jon's philosophy was more about how things sounded. So it was more the sound of the vocal that he was trying to always write for, as opposed to the actual logical sense of the lyric (laughs). And so, for years, of course, I was singing harmonies with sentences that didn't mean a thing, really, but sounded good (laughs). Yes' philosophy, by the name alone, was always to have a positive influence. We weren't as concerned with the dark side of rock 'n' roll as a lot of artists are. And a lot of people like that. Yes always had that philosophy of hope and a brighter future."
**Chris Squire**

# 1977: Going for the One

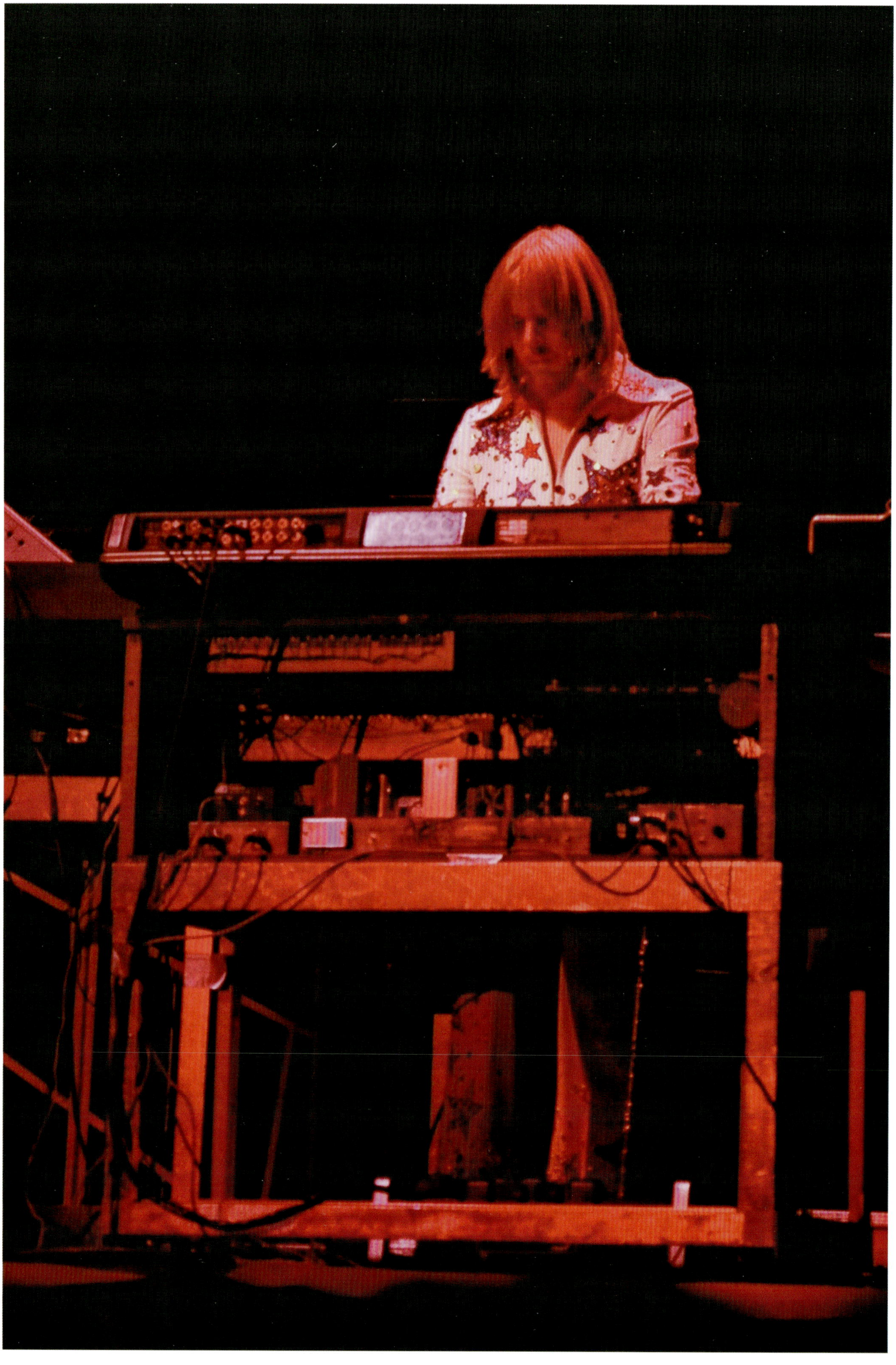

Back to work in '77, post-*Relayer*, Yes was smart enough or restless enough or impatient enough to try something new when it came time for them to answer for their sweet an' sour, hard-rocking jazz fusion album with the snake on the cover. Rick Wakeman had returned on keyboards, and brought with him the chemistry he had taken away, as well as his sociability and joviality, and the result was a confident, ebullient triumph of a record called *Going for the One*. As a result, Yes would still fly high, ever-present in the press, treated with a degree of respect (even though they would never particularly get across to the likes of *Rolling Stone* and *Creem*), and more importantly, continue to expand the minds of millions of fans per year, all during the sullen hot summer of the Pistols and The Clash.

Elsewhere Patrick Moraz bounces back (as does another past tickler of the ivories Tony Kaye) while something called The Buggles takes shape. We'll leave it at that, because coming up is my own long review of the band's momentous offering from this year, *Going for the One* in fact being my favourite Yes album of all time (as reiterated on an episode of my Youtube show The Contrarians).

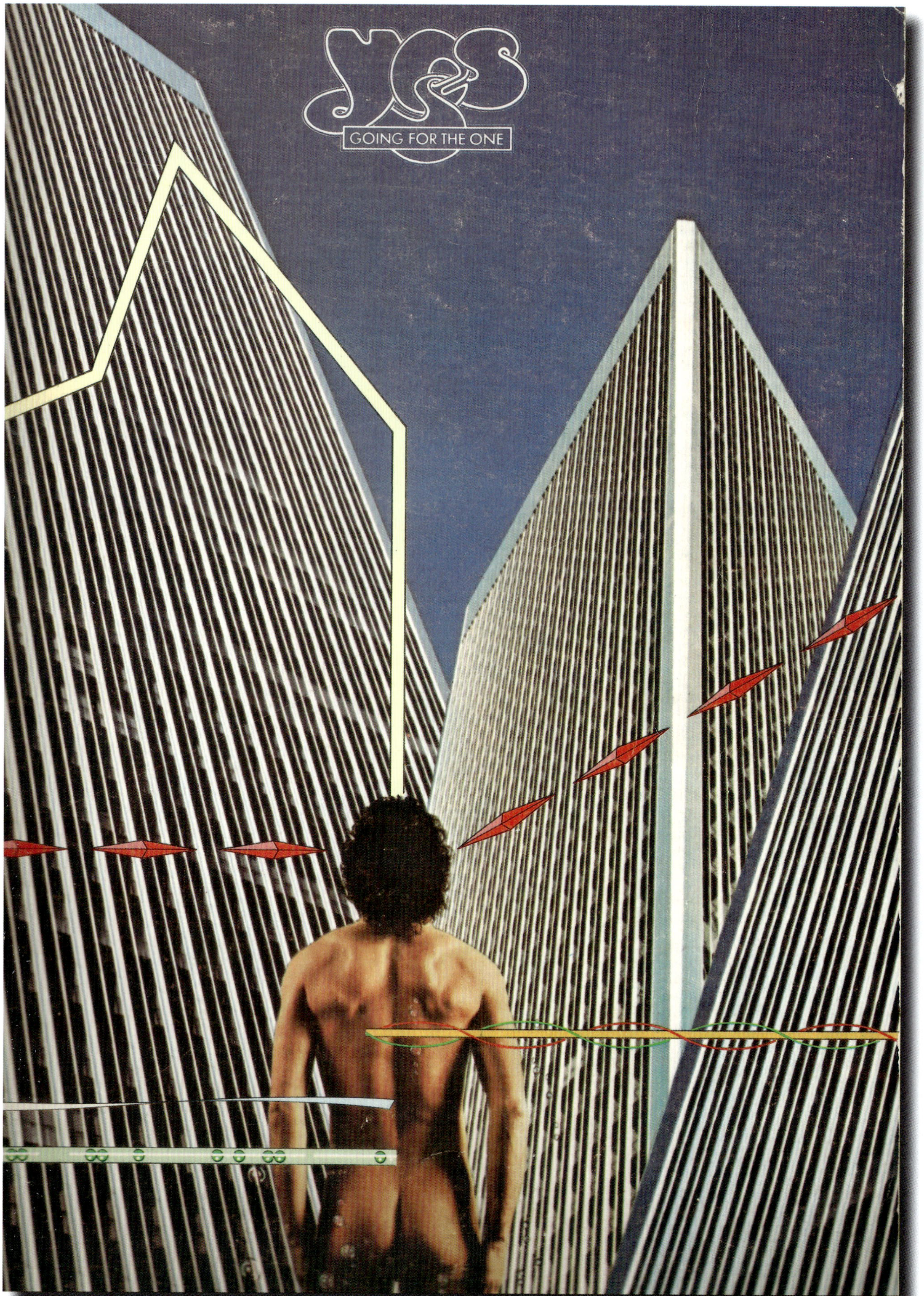
YES
GOING FOR THE ONE

**1977.** Geoff Downes and Trevor Horn form pioneering electronic post-punk duo The Buggles. Managing the band would be Brian Lane, also manager of Yes.

> *Geoff Downes on his prog pedigree despite forming The Buggles:*
> *"'Round about the time that* Close to the Edge *came out, I had just started at music college. So I was very much into Yes at that point. I really liked,* Time and a Word, The Yes Album, Close to the Edge, Fragile; *those were very much albums I listened to in that period in music college. But by '76, '77, I started to work more towards different types of music. I did a lot of session work in London doing mainly disco and dance stuff, and that's how I met Trevor Horn, because there was quite a well-known disco singer called Tina Charles at the time, and he got together with them, and I auditioned for the band, and that's how we got together. So at that point, we were into more mainstream pop stuff, more to do with the fact that we were making a living out of it, than we were going to make a living playing music that we particularly liked. It was more the fact that we were doing stuff that was keeping us alive."*

**January 2, 1977.** Patrick Moraz, now ousted from Yes, gets busy down in Rio de Janeiro on his next solo album, slated for an April release (but then delayed).

**Early 1977.** Tony Kaye resurfaces in Swan Song Records supergroup Detective, who issue a self-titled record followed by *It Takes One to Know One* later in the same year. He's the band's keyboardist but only gets two songwriting credits across the two albums.

**April 8, 1977.** The Clash issue their angry and ground-breaking self-titled debut and Yes suddenly looks like a luxury item.

**July 7, 1977.** Yes, issue their eighth studio album, *Going for the One*, a record that is both commercially successful and well received by the fans, demonstrating that punk isn't everybody's cup of tea. The album, late in the shops by seven months, reaches No.1 in the UK, and peaks at No.8 in the US, on the strength of singles "Wonderous Stories" and "Going for the One." The album achieves gold certification in the US within a month of release. For cover art, the band go for a modern approach, eschewing fantastical illustration for a sleek sleeve by Hipgnosis, who will be on board for the follow-up as well.

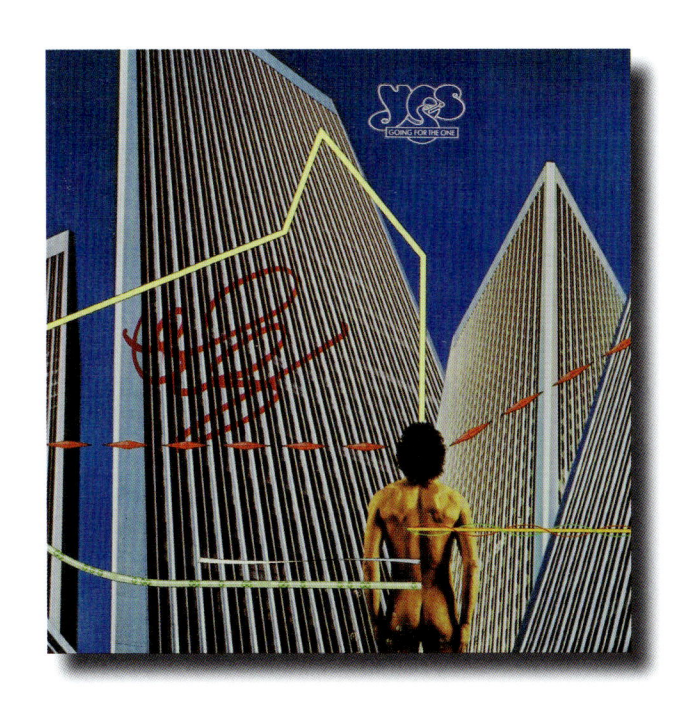

### Jon Anderson, in 1977:

"This album is a kind of celebration. Over the last two or three years, we've been experimenting a lot, and we're happy to have been given that chance. Any musician should be given the chance to extend his horizons and luckily we've been successful enough to do so. We think of this as a more eventful album. We've come back to a happier medium. It's something we felt we wanted to do. If we wanted another Tales concept, we would've gone in that direction, but we needed to relax for a while—a little more laughing and jive."

### Rick Wakeman:

"We both, me and the band, did a different journey around an egg to arrive at Going for the One, which was great. I suppose if you have to pick pieces that are immensely highlights for me, it would have to be 'Awaken.' I still think that's a Yes anthem. If anybody ever asks me, what is Yes all about? I say, well, if you listen to 'Awaken,' that gives you a pretty good clue."

### Steve Howe:

"'Awaken' is really an Anderson/Howe song, but because the guys did a great job on arranging it, we included them in on the arrangement. They didn't actually write the song but we put their names on the song and that's because you can't kind of give and take away at the same time. If you're going to give credit to somebody, then you have to give it to them, and it rewards them. On the other hand, sometimes it does sort of mystify the actual writer credit. Jon and I always assumed that 'Awaken' would say Anderson/Howe, and it doesn't."

### Alan White on Jon Anderson's world view:

"A lot of the older material was driven, in that sense, by Jon, with his exploration of spiritualism and surreal situations, and using his voice like an instrument more than anything, within the whole mixture, where he let the audience translate what it meant. Because it could conjure up a lot of different things. Yes had that mystique about it right from the early days. But the message of the band is, just we keep on going, trying to create music that no one else is playing. You can always tell a Yes song on the radio."

### Author review:

"As would be the case a presidential term hence, Yes signal a new era with bold new graphics. Gone is the swirly escapism of Roger Dean; in its place, a new accelerated, late-'70s escapism through the clean lines of Hipgnosis, who combine slick, futuristic geometric urban angles with man in birthday suit, perhaps urgently propelling the band forward, while simultaneously embracing roots. Whatever the case, Going for the One becomes a splendidly well-written, instantly likeable progressive rock record, a balance rarely attained by anyone, a balance Yes has known on their three great records from years earlier, The Yes Album, Fragile and Close to the Edge."

"The album's kick-off track is indeed a kick, Yes surprising everyone with a rousing, jaunty bit of Foghat boogie. When the shameless Americanizing evaporates, soaring, sun-dappled cathedrals spring from the soil, Yes inventing perhaps the most compelling short track of their career, replete with vocals from (the circus of) heaven, heaps o' Howe slide, and well, rock 'n' roll! Firmly ensconced as a concert fave, 'Going for the One' is a lusty lead track indeed, announcing that the bewildered wilderness of Tales from Topographic Oceans and Relayer has been energetically clear-cut to make room for beefy cattle."

"Next up, with 'Turn of the Century,' things became more ethereal and light, Jon adapting the La Boheme tale of a sculptor molding his love for his departed soul mate into his work. Steve and Jon trade textures throughout the touching first half, the track building, first with bass and peaceful keyboard washes, then with more effortlessly integrated strata of the same, adding Alan's timpani and soft cymbal crashes. All told, it's a gorgeous, deceptively full-bodied track, the ultimate demonstration of dynamic sonic layering."

"And in crashes 'Parallels,' Wakeman droning forth with powerful church organ chords from

St. Martin's Church in Montreux, on what is a rousing Chris Squire composition, again filled with texture of a very different sort. Wakeman's organ virtually acts as bass guitar, as Squire straddles bass patterns to soloing, and Howe exclusively colours as soloist. Indeed riff and bass both seem to be the swallowed domain of Wakeman, as Jon belts out an uncharacteristically lucid tale of betterment over the mistaken identities of his band mates. It's a rocker for sure, and as much as 'Going for the One,' a metaphor for the waking-up of good feeling the band was experiencing at the time (and Wakeman gets to belt out a solo eventually)."

"Side two opens with yet another Yes classic of a more benign stripe, 'Wonderous Stories' being perhaps the most beautiful Yes composition of the quiet sort, an angelic acoustic bit of frolic, whose deceptive, simple arrangement bears many hard-won treasures. Anderson is truly dramatic in his presentation of this tale reaching back into times classical, renaissance, and wonderous (sic). Like 'Turn of the Century,' its build is subversive and effortless, Alan White's percussion truly that, percussion that accents and shades, all the while Wakeman slowly filling up all until the heaven-sent environs is achieved come climactic round by Jon and Jon and Jon."

"Closing the show is 'Awaken,' an involved composition that harkens back to any kitchen sink Yes prog monster one can imagine. All aspects of this very difficult track are bewildering, from Jon's supposed lyrical sources (timeless song cycles, Rembrandt, classical music, Topographic Oceans), to Wakeman's recording of his pipe organ parts over Switzerland's sonically super-efficient phone lines."

"The deposed Patrick Moraz, who was very instrumental in the writing of the album as a whole, feels most slighted by his being uncredited here on 'Awaken,' the piece on the record he felt was most his. And given that his contributions were surgically but somewhat subconsciously removed, the track does sound a little forced, a little too eventful and segued. But those wishing to hear a superhuman Yes labyrinth for '77 found themselves floored or at least satiated."

"All told, Going for the One is a fun record, reversing the furrowed seriousness of the last two slabs of pain. Switzerland helped, but so did the return of Wakeman, who added oddball spice to the sessions. Once he was back as full collaborator and Yes member, his ideas proved tantamount. Keyboards of many stripes are all over this record, yet a raw, rock 'n' roll guitars and vocals record is what springs to mind first."

### Journalist John Swenson:
"As the band continued to run through the possible program readouts, less and less creative energy became available and Yes sank into cosmic torpor. Going for the One reverses this process in a fascinating move that ties them even more closely to Zeppelin. By letting the Chris Squire-Alan White rhythm section construct a bottom for Howe's guitar, and by using Wakeman's unquestionable keyboard talent intelligently, Going for the One takes the right step toward downplaying Anderson's conceptual stranglehold on the band. Entropy can work to your advantage. You just have to be selective about where the energy is taken from."

**July 30 – December 6, 1977.** Yes mount their *Going for the One* tour, with Donovan as support.

### Alan White:
"Going for the One was a memorable experience for everybody in the band. It was a period when Rick came back to the band and we were all excited about that and we just enjoyed living in Switzerland together. I think we were there, six, seven, eight months, in the winter. We'd turn up at the studio every day, and everybody had fun creating this wonderful album. And it's a great album to play on stage, particularly 'Awaken.' The song itself, 'Going for the One,' a lot of people, really, really love that song. And 'Turn of the Century' is one of the more difficult pieces for us to play on stage, and that's a song I did with Jon Anderson. You've really got to be on top to play that on stage. A lot of the parts don't have any time signatures, so you have to listen really intently to what the other guys are playing."

146

July 30th, 1977, Toledo Sports Arena, Toledo, OH.

**August 1977.** Patrick Moraz issues, on Charisma Records, a solo album called *Out in the Sun*. Front and centre in the author's rock 'n' roll display case are the promotional *Out in the Sun* sunglasses. Many more solo albums would follow, but of note would be Moraz' 13-year run with prog pioneers The Moody Blues.

**September 1977.** "Wonderous Stories"/"Parallels" is issued in the UK as 7", 12" and blue 12" vinyl single form, reaching No.7 in the charts. The American version of "Wonderous Stories" is backed with an abbreviated "Awaken." As well, "Wonderous Stories," presented in fairly rudimentary live format, stands as the band's first single track production video.

### Jon Anderson, in 1977, on "Wonderous Stories:"
*"It was a beautiful day in Switzerland. It was one of those days you want to remember for years afterwards. The words 'wonderous stories' came into my head. It's an exuberant song and that's really the whole theme for our album Going for the One. The tracks have lots of potential energy but some of them fade into the relaxation of triumph you must feel after a marathon event. The album reflects achievement like the Olympics or skiing. There's a guy who's skied down a mountain in Japan. Imagine how that must feel. The album has a happy feeling as well because it's a reunion with Rick. Before we recorded Going for the One I suggested we should have him back and he came down one afternoon and we jammed together for hours. I think Patrick Moraz felt his experience with Yes was extremely valuable and worthwhile. He did very well but there was a certain amount of drifting apart. Yet we all parted friends."*

### Rick Wakeman, in 1977:
*"The new album bears no resemblance to the last couple of albums—it's all songs again. It's a rock 'n' roll song album. In the same way that I had to leave— because I couldn't bear playing anymore— in order to find out that these were the people I wanted to play with, we now happen to think we make pretty good music together."*

### Steve Howe, in 1977:
*"It takes discussion, strictness and ambition! Ambition is one of the heaviest driving forces. It's not a matter of aggression, but freedom to comment about what's going on. There was a fair bit of go and aggression in the music I was first involved in, with The In Crowd and Tomorrow. In those groups, we wanted to tear the people apart! And Yes were doing that too, in their early days. Because of our achievements later, we began to go off at a tangent and become mellow. 'Going for the One' on the album was a rebirth of that fire."*

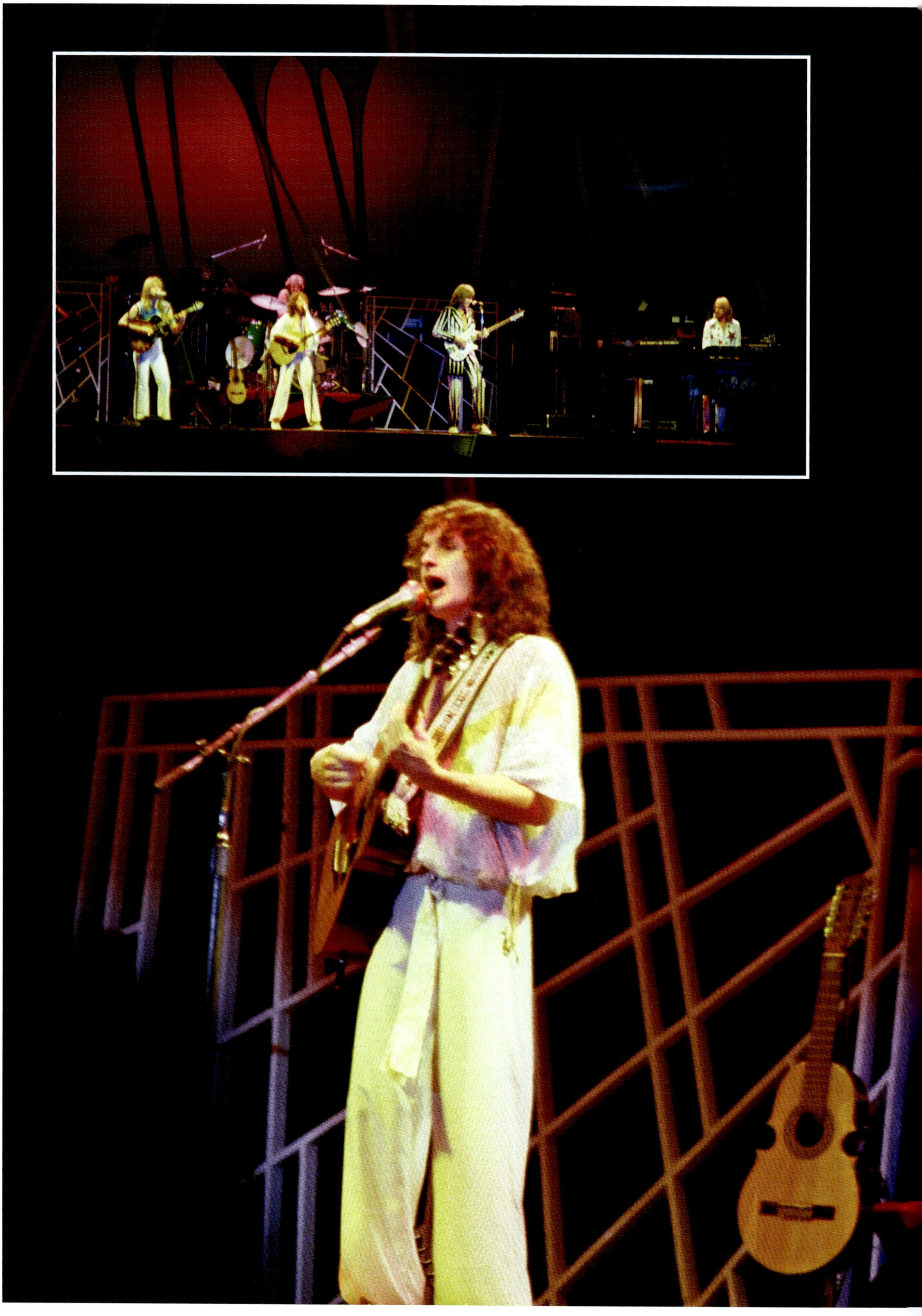

October 26th, 1977, Empire Pool, Wembley.

© Alan Perry

152

October 26th, 1977, Empire Pool, Wembley.

# YES

JULY 2, 1977, BILLBOARD

SPECIAL GUEST STAR
## DONOVAN

## SOLD OUT
## 4 MONTHS IN ADVANCE

*Thank you*

**FRIDAY, SATURDAY, SUNDAY, AUGUST 5, 6, 7 — 8 PM**

**madison square garden**
Pennsylvania Plaza 7th Ave. 31st to 33rd Sts.

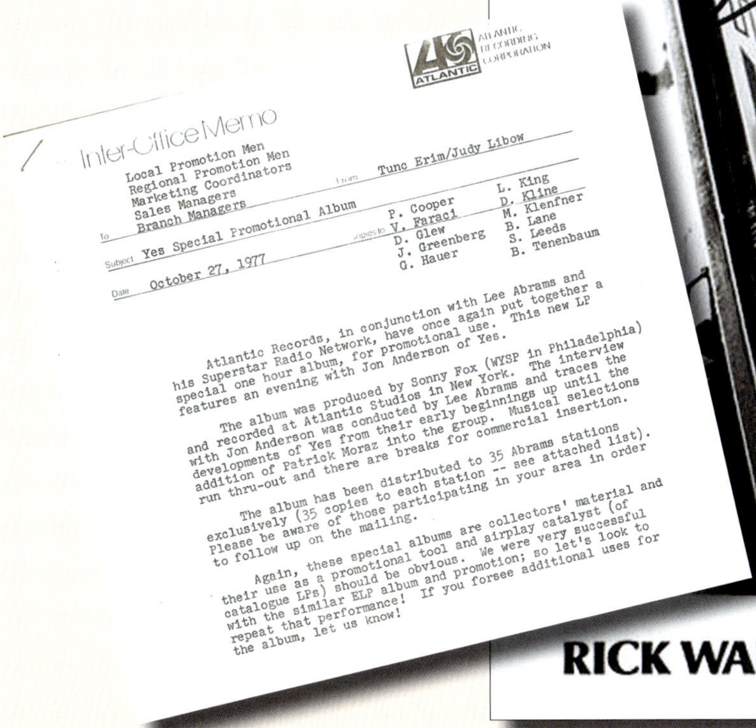

ATLANTIC RECORDING CORPORATION

Inter-Office Memo

To: Local Promotion Men
Regional Promotion Men
Marketing Coordinators
Sales Managers
Branch Managers

From: Tunc Erim/Judy Libow

Subject: Yes Special Promotional Album

Copies to: P. Cooper, V. Faraci, D. Glew, J. Greenberg, G. Hauer, L. King, D. Kline, M. Klenfner, B. Lane, S. Leeds, B. Tenenbaum

Date: October 27, 1977

Atlantic Records, in conjunction with Lee Abrams and his Superstar Radio Network, have once again put together a special one hour album, for promotional use. This new LP features an evening with Jon Anderson of Yes.

The album was produced by Sonny Fox (WYSP in Philadelphia) and recorded at Atlantic Studios in New York. The interview with Jon Anderson was conducted by Lee Abrams and traces the developments of Yes from their early beginnings up until the addition of Patrick Moraz into the group. Musical selections run thru-out and there are breaks for commercial insertion.

The album has been distributed to 35 Abrams stations exclusively (35 copies to each station -- see attached list). Please be aware of those participating in your area in order to follow up on the mailing.

Again, these special albums are collectors' material and their use as a promotional tool and airplay catalyst (of catalogue LPs) should be obvious. We were very successful with the similar ELP album and promotion; so let's look to repeat that performance! If you forsee additional uses for the album, let us know!

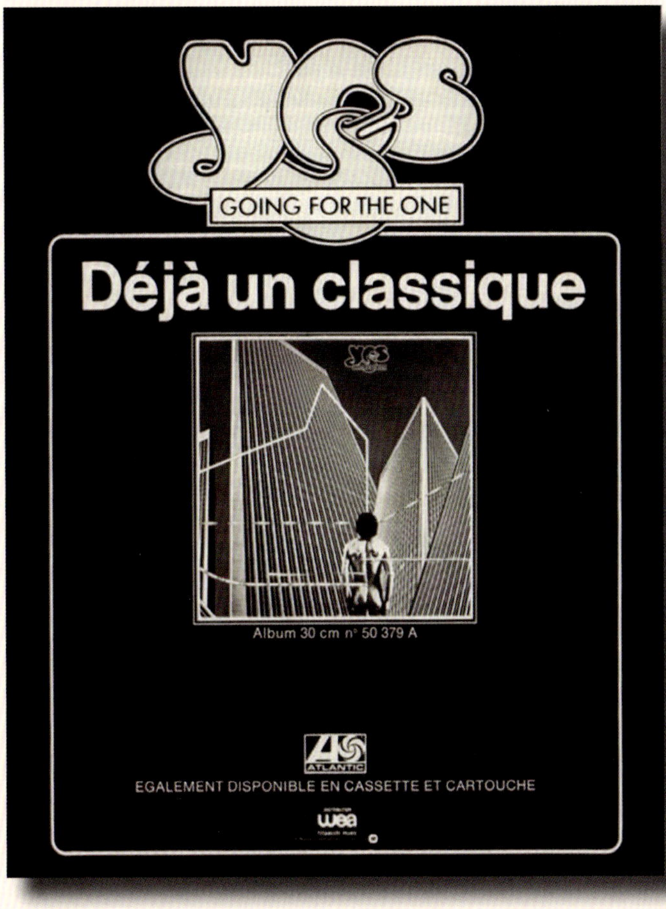

"I'm not really a defender of *Tormato*, no. I think the weaknesses in that record are the first time we really had trouble in tone, in quality of sound—that was there. But this is because the group was starting to produce ourselves, each other and ourselves. It was a difficult time because for me it's particularly nice when Rick and I aren't competing, with me on an electric guitar and him on a synthesizer. Because right at that time, that was when the guitar and synthesizer sounds weren't mixing well. He was playing a thing called a Polymoog which he loved to bits, and he had his Birotron or something. He loved all those things, which we did as well. But in particular the Polymoog was very destructive towards guitar. I would play something and he would play something and they would kind of cancel each other out. That was one of the weaknesses."
**Steve Howe**

# 1978 to 1979: *Tormato*

166

September 6th, 1978, Madison Square Garden, New York.

© Frank White

September 29th, 1978, Tulsa Assembly Center, Tulsa, OK.

© Rich Galbraith

September 29th, 1978, Tulsa Assembly Center, Tulsa, OK.

© Rich Galbraith

© Rich Galbraith

181

September 29th, 1978, Tulsa Assembly Center, Tulsa, OK.

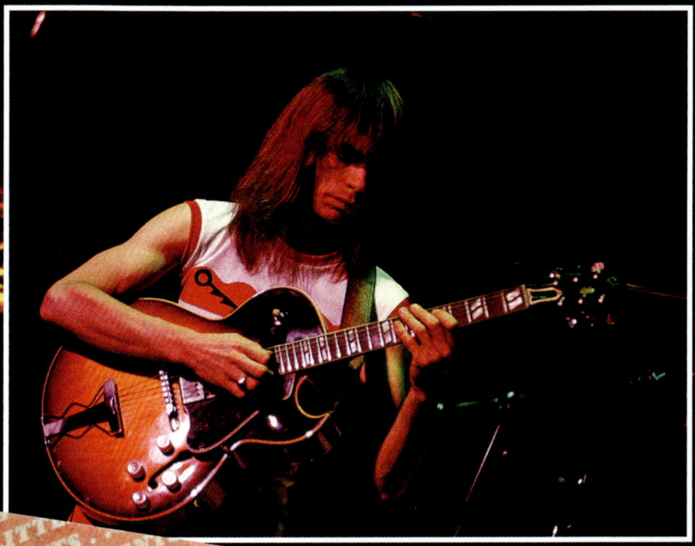

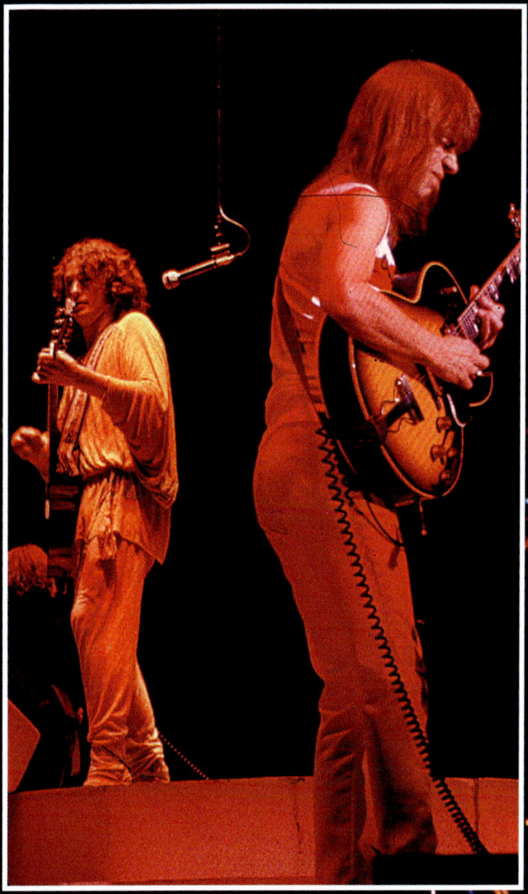

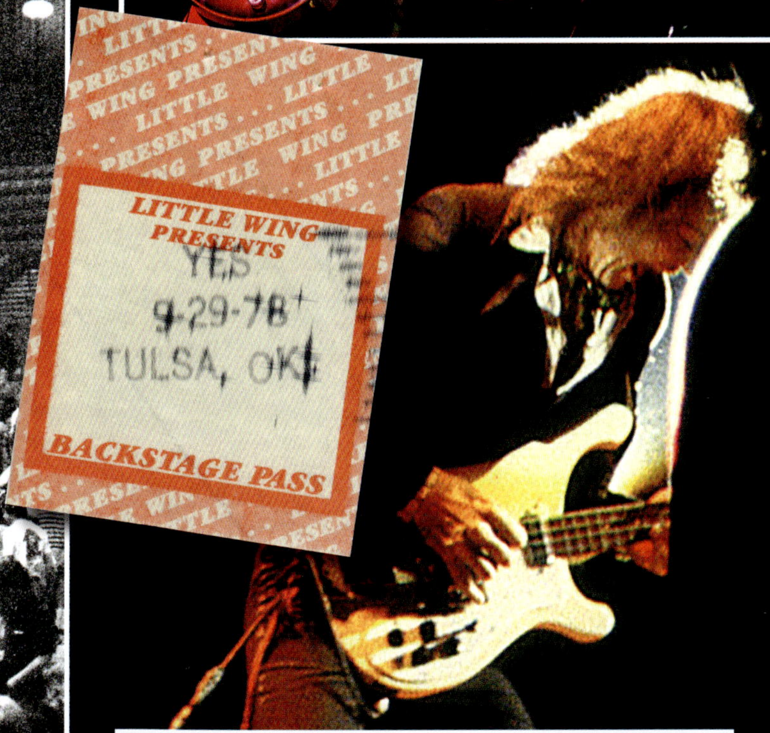
LITTLE WING
PRESENTS
YES
9-29-78
TULSA, OK
BACKSTAGE PASS

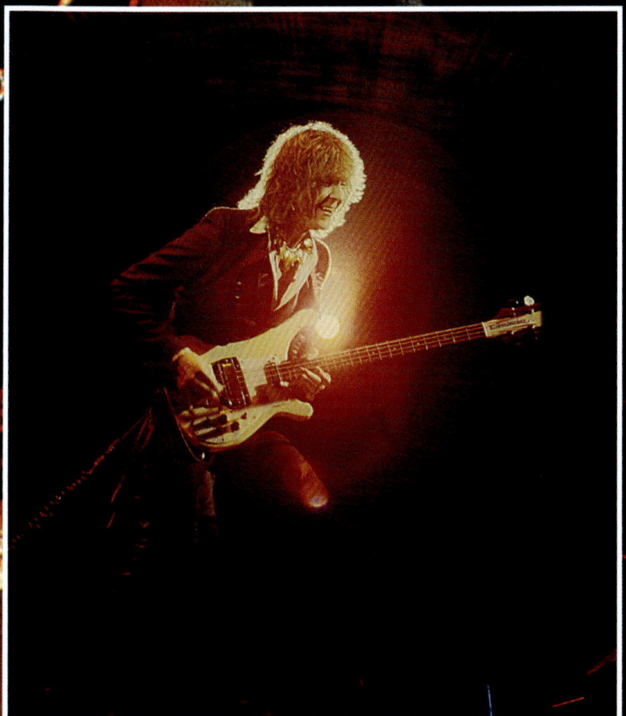

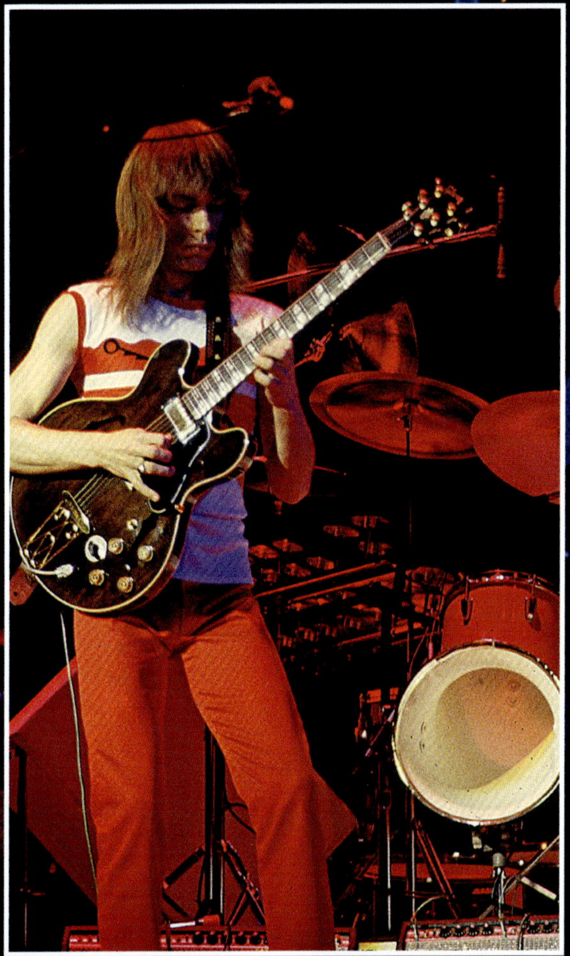

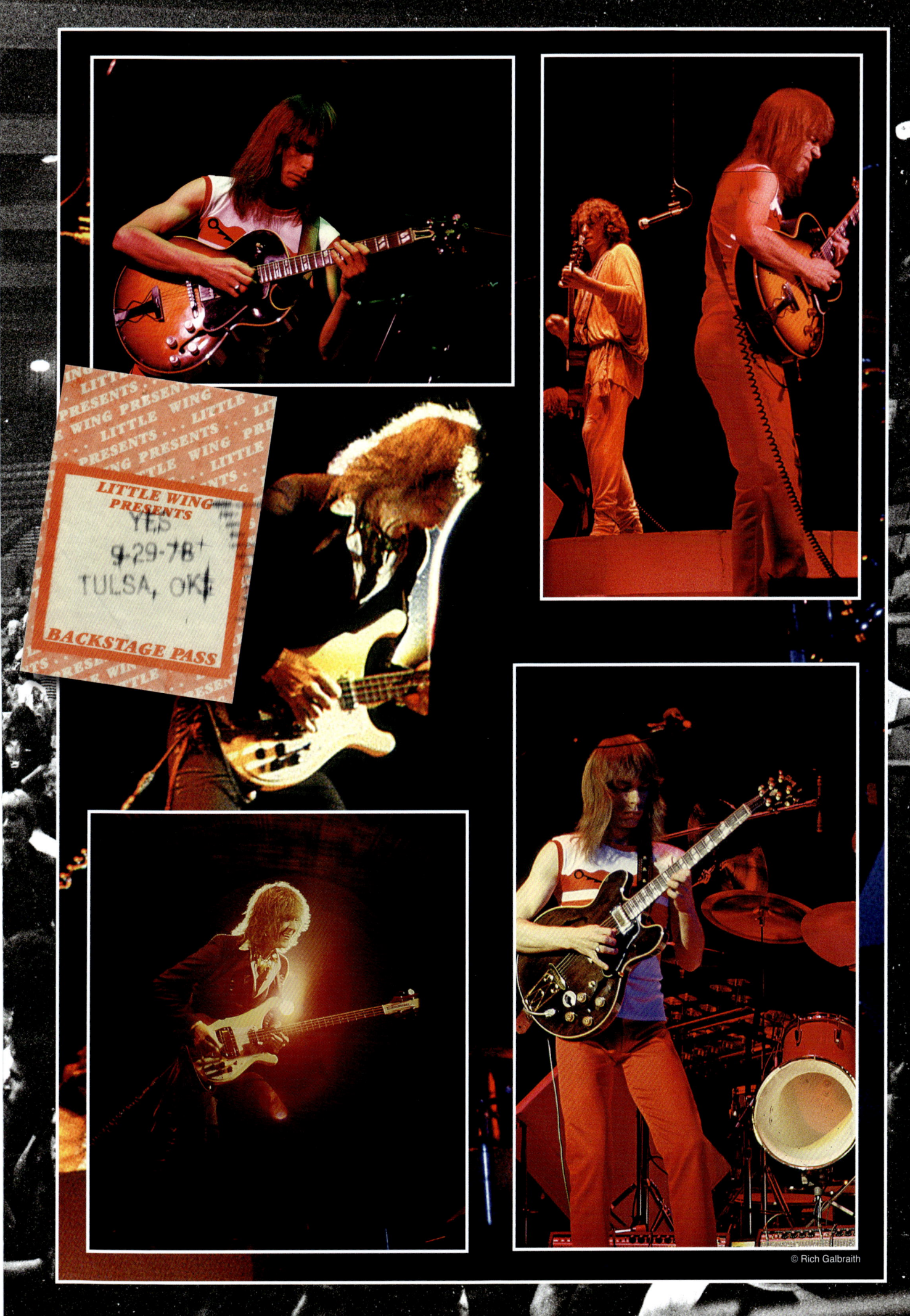

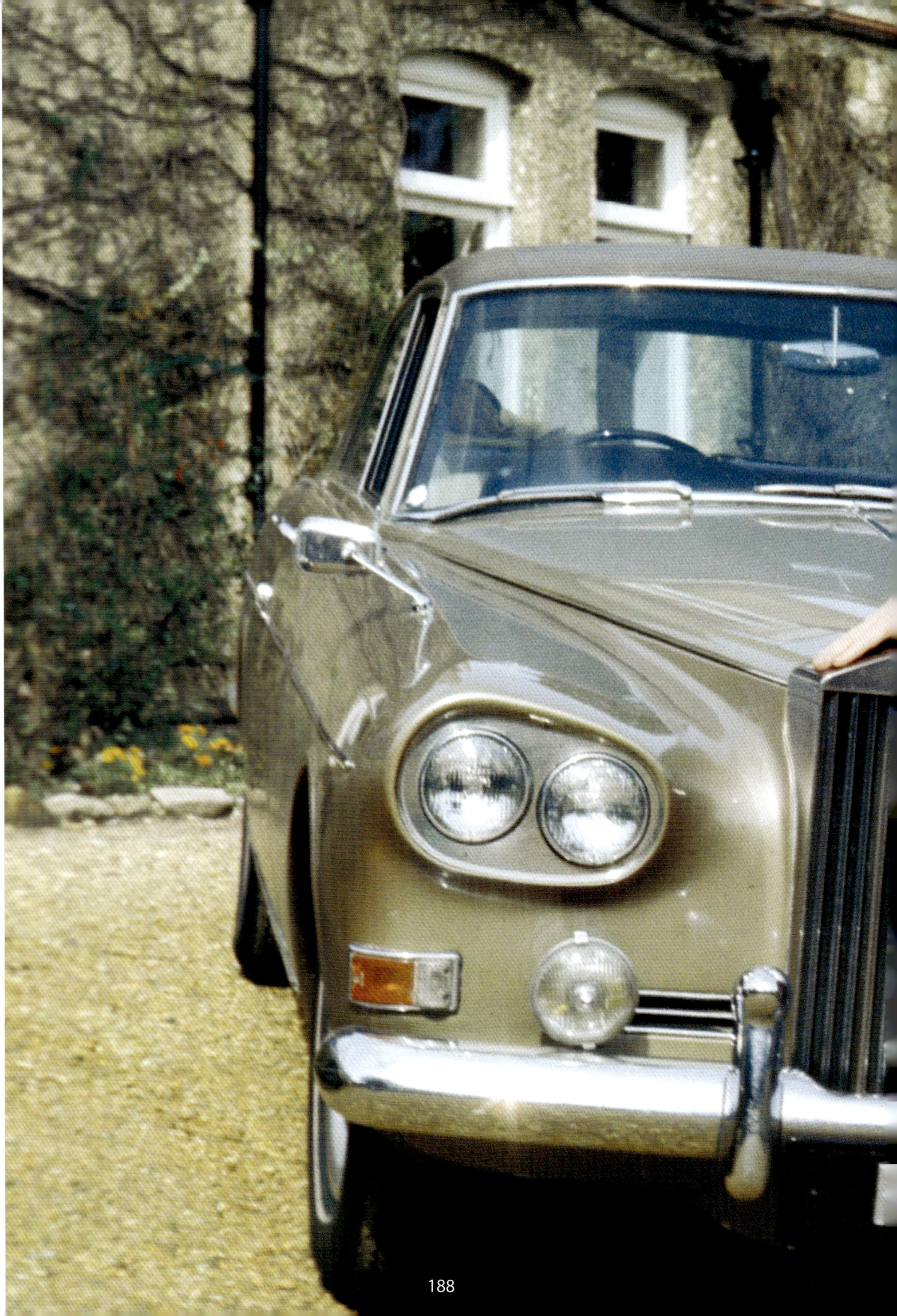

Rick has always had a passion for cars and the success of Yes, as well as his solo career, afforded him the luxury to indulge.

"When we made the first Buggles album, me and Trevor were not really known at all by anybody. We were just a couple of guys making music, and jobbing producers and session musicians. So it was a big change when we finished that first album, which was very successful, obviously, with 'Video Killed the Radio Star' being on MTV. So it was very successful for us, and I think that was one of the reasons why that got the guys in Yes at the time excited, was that we were breaking new boundaries and pushing the envelope, in terms of making music."
Geoff Downes

# 1980 to 1981: *Drama*

September 4th, 1980,
Madison Square Garden,
New York.

Theoretically, Yes should have been killed off so that rock in the '80s could operate unhindered by 18-minute-long multi-disciplinary spiritual quests set to music only deciphered with calculator and slide rule. Punk, long dead, became post-punk in the UK, and in the US, a cheerier, more palatable and amorphous non-category known as New Wave. We also saw a healthy industry in music made primarily by synthesizers and other adjunct technology, to the point where a debate was being had for real whether rock was dead, and indeed, whether computers could completely replace people in the creation of music.

As well, there was a New Wave of British Heavy Metal circa 1980 to 1983, which sparked a massive interest in heavy metal in Los Angeles in the mid '80s, with heavy music evolving into thrash on the harsh side and hair metal on the more accessible other. Filling the gap between those two, most hard rock dinosaurs of the '70s were now doing even better business than they did back then, codified in the arid heat of California on Heavy Metal Day at the US Festival circa 1983.

And where did Yes fit in all this? Well, practical businessmen that they are, they bellied back to the bar with an album called *Drama* in 1980, which found Rick Wakeman replaced by Geoff Downes, but infinitely more of a travesty, Jon Anderson replaced on vocals by Trevor Horn. Fan acceptance of the album was stronger than fan acceptance of the band live, but even so, the meticulously crafted, audiophile-quality record was pretty much ignored. Over time, it's gotten its just due, and *Drama* is now considered by most Yes fans as a very fine Yes album indeed.

© Bill O'Leary

**1980.** Rick Wakeman marries for the second time. The marriage to Danielle lasts but a year, producing one child.

**January 1980.** Jon and Vangelis issue their debut, on Polydor, called *Short Stories*.

**January 10, 1980.** The Buggles issue their debut album, on Island, called *The Age of Plastic*. The band is a duo, consisting of future Yes members, Trevor Horn and Geoff Downes. The album hatches a smash single called "Video Killed the Radio Star," which hits No.1 in the UK and No.40 in the US.

> *Trevor Horn on calling the band The Buggles:*
> "We were getting the third degree from other labels that wanted to know if we were going to tour, if The Buggles was a band. In fact, when we took the demo around, we weren't a band at all. It was a studio concept. You see, as producers, we had become very cynical about names, about categorisation. We decided to find a name that was a horror and The Buggles fitted the tag perfectly. If anything, the name is a play on an electronic bug. But then again, The Buggles means absolutely nothing."

**April – June 1980.** Yes works on what will be their first album without Jon Anderson as lead vocalist, and without long-time keyboardist Rick Wakeman. A Buggles song is offered by Trevor for possibly inclusion on the new Yes record. With Trevor and Geoff Downes in the studio with Yes to help them get the song straight, the absence of Rick and Jon is immediately noted and soon the duo are asked to join the band. The suggestion comes from Chris, who had struck up a friendship with the guys through their mutually shared management.

> *Alan White:*
> "That lineup was really started by Steve, Chris, and myself. Jon wasn't involved at that time, and we just went into rehearsals and to Munich with the idea to do a new album. In the next studio was Trevor Horn and Geoff Downes, and they were fans of the band, and they kept coming in and listening to us. Finally one day Trevor said, 'I've written a song that you guys can do really well,' and then all of a sudden we were playing the song and they're both kind of in Yes. We had a meeting, and then we went in the studio and recorded. That was another album where a lot of people brought a lot of music from a lot of different areas; it was compiled really by all of us, and we had a great time. I think it's an underrated album, one of the band's better albums."

> *Geoff Downes:*
> "A lot of people like Drama. It showed that Yes were prepared to access and push new boundaries. From my standpoint, a piece like 'Machine Messiah' is a worthy contender to sit along with some of the best Yes stuff. It has the hallmarks of a Yes piece, as does the whole album, which doesn't really sound like anybody else. It sounds very disciplined as a record but actually we were all over the place in terms of recording. I mean, that's why the album name Drama came up, because the amalgamation of the other three guys and me and Trevor was not holding great reverence in some corners, certainly with the diehard Yes fans."
>
> "But I think once they got to hear the album, and over time, people have warmed to it. It was put together with a lot of rehearsing and care. Eddie Offord came for some of it, and then he left, and we had to finish it off on our own. It ended up as a kind of group-produced album. Eddie Offord did the backing tracks, but everything else was done as a group production. That's where it usually can sound absolutely awful, where the band are all hanging over the faders. But it actually does stand up and sounds pretty powerful and punchy still. So it had a lot of ups and downs, but if you look at it in the cold light of day, it's a solid album."

September 4th, 1980,
Madison Square Garden,
New York.

© Frank White

September 4th, 1980,
Madison Square Garden,
New York.

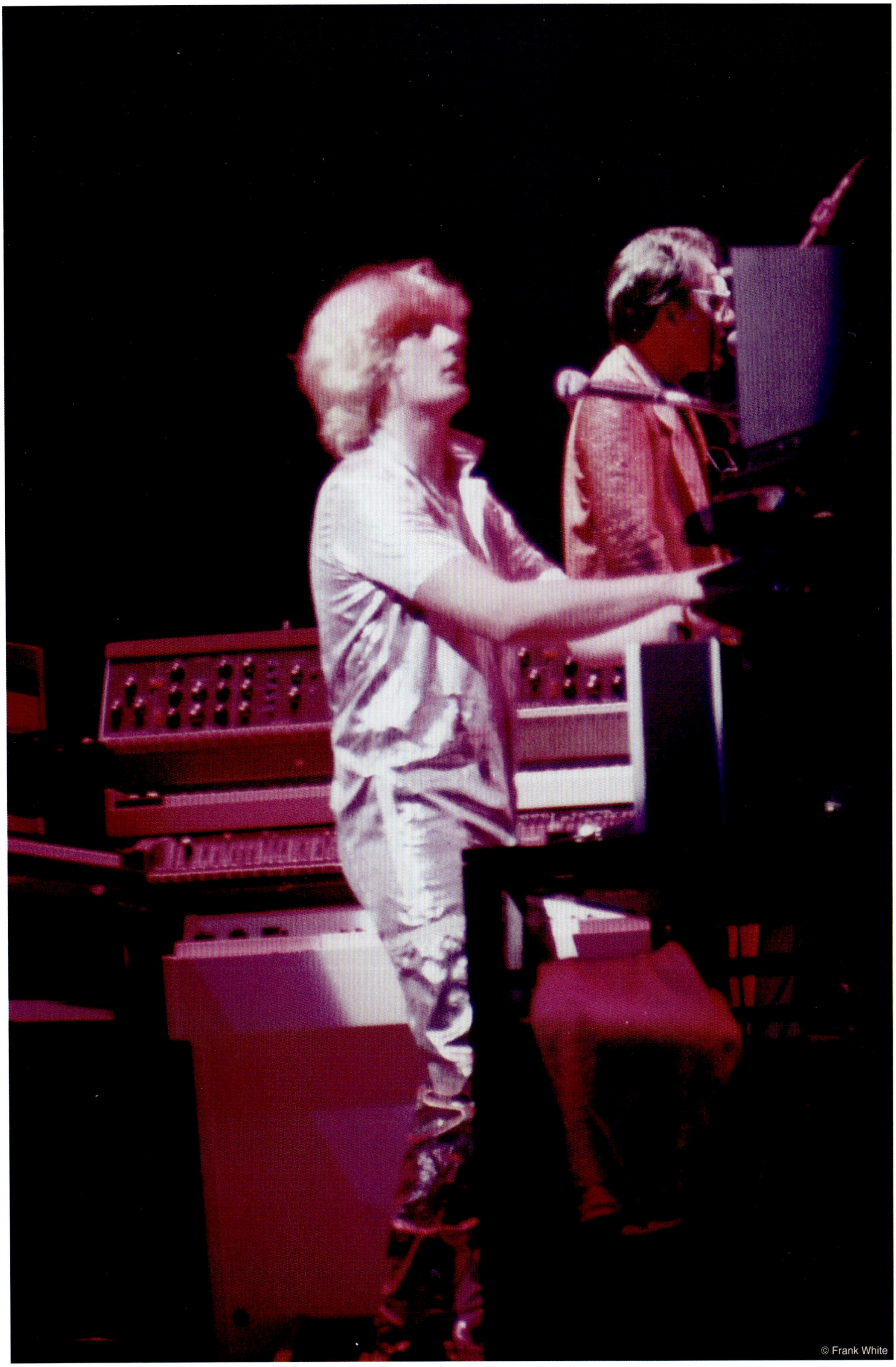
© Frank White

206

September 6th, 1980,
Madison Square Garden,
New York.

September 6th, 1980,
Madison Square Garden,
New York.

© Bill O´Leary

September 6th, 1980,
Madison Square Garden,
New York.

© Bill O'Leary

© Bill O'Leary

*Author review:*

*"Years since his last solo flight, Jon Anderson is in a very difficult frame of mind. No longer defined by Yes, Jon spices this truly solo, truly on-yer-own record with oscillations between fresh optimism, soul-searching panic and stale regression. The overall vibe however leans towards hope, if tinged with escapism, Jon assembling a hybrid of shameless, mystical hippie musings, bouncy R&B rhythms and occasional new-ish electronic technologies (see the anthemic 'For You for Me'). But even that catch-all refuses to catch all, 'Hear It' and 'Days' harkening back to the fireside madrigal feel of Olias, 'Don't Forget (Nostalgia)' half-heartedly courting the blues, and 'Heart of the Matter' sounding like something off of Sesame Street."*

*"The biggest advance however, is the fact that Song of Seven is a full-band record, most noticeable performances being the electric jazz/Jeff Berlin stylings of John Giblin (he is one of four bassists on the project), and the sax work of Dick Morrissey, who adds a Young Americans dimension to the lighter, bouncier side one."*

*"But come side two, Jon tends to slip back into his acoustic prog cocoon, blowing the record out with the 11-minute title track, a sort of delicate Yes pageant with too much emotion and therefore a belittling of emotion through over-beratement, Jon and his band of strangers functioning as Starcastle. Sum total of the Song of Seven experience? One of fragmentation (think Peter Gabriel's first two records, or the Ian Gillan Band), too many disparate pop rock styles, long tracks next to short, the only constant being Anderson's unflagging spiritualism, a bright light that illuminates every track with hope, despite often maudlin musical beds on which that hope bounces like a toddler."*

**November 12 – December 16, 1980.** Jon Anderson plays one date in Germany and five in the UK in support of *Song of Seven*. The band is billed as Jon Anderson with the New Life Band.

**November 24, 1980.** Yes issue their second live album, a two LP set called *Yesshows*. Although released after *Drama*, the album features Jon Anderson on vocals, given that it is composed of performances from 1976 through 1978. Indeed the band had scheduled the recording and issuing of a double live album back on the *Going for the One* tour, planning to use shows from the tour leg in Australia and Japan. Many shows in fact were recorded, with plans also set at that time for a feature documentary on the band.

**December 1980.** Yes is for all intents and purposes broken up. Meanwhile, Geffen A&R wizard John Kalodner envisions a new prog supergroup, now that both U.K. and Yes are no more. Brian Lane, first fired by The Buggles and then Yes, within a few weeks is on board as the manager of Steve's and Geoff's bright new idea, which at that point had included a bass player as well named John Wetton. Eventually joining would be Carl Palmer (progressive rock's version of Cozy Powell), but not before Simon Phillips (a baby Bill Bruford in both looks and sound) had been suggested for the drum stool.

### Trevor Rabin:

*"I was producing Manfred Mann at the time and that is how I met Kalodner. He had never heard of me as a guitar player, so I sent him some stuff. I actually met David Geffen, who I met first, as we went out to lunch. A few weeks later, Kalodner had me getting my stuff together to move. I was given a development deal in order to write music for an album that I thought was going to be a solo album. Kalodner told me in order to go the fast route I should join some other known musicians and write some music with them. He told me doing a solo album would be much harder. I met with Carl Palmer and we got on quite well. John Wetton then came in to try out as a bass player."*

*"Some time went by and I didn't hear anything for a few months. Kalodner phoned me one day and said, 'Look, I've got this thing with Steve Howe, Carl Palmer and Geoff Downes. We would very much like you to go and check it out.' I said, 'I don't want to have some big name supergroup-type of vibe that eclipses anything musical.' I was very cynical about it and I didn't want to do it. Kalodner told me, 'You've got to do this or we will be dropping you.' I said, 'Fine.' I went and I just hated it. From their point of view, they really didn't need me, as they were great. I think we had two days of rehearsal and I went back to John and I stuck to my guns and said I was not doing that. It was quite amazing—two days later I got a call that I was dropped. I should have done it (laughs)."*

### Geoff Downes on why Yes disintegrated after Drama:

*"It happened largely because I don't think Trevor was that comfortable being the lead vocalist. We finished in the UK, and he wasn't really enjoying it that much. He felt that it wasn't really for him. He wanted to be more of a record producer, which, I think he made the right choice, because he's an incredible record producer. Time and time again, he's done some groundbreaking albums over the years with a variety of artists. But it had been difficult because Trevor himself was not actually a singer's singer. He was a bass player really, and singing was something else that he did. It wasn't really his instrument. Under the circumstances, he carried himself particularly well, especially on the record."*

*"But by the time we came to do the dates, it was much more difficult. Because someone like Anderson sings for two, two-and-a-half hours every night and doesn't miss a note. It's also very high register. For someone to come in and carry that off, I'm surprised that Trevor actually did it as well as he did. It's a formidable prospect. I think the UK tour particularly, Trevor got a lot of stick from the Yes fans here. People were more understanding and prepared to listen in America, but I think here there was a lot of prejudice that me and him had come into this situation and were not suitable replacements for Anderson and Wakeman. So after that UK tour, Trevor felt, look, I can't carry on with this, and I was pretty much of the same opinion. So that's when we went back and started to do another Buggles album."*

**1981** Alan White marries Gigi. Still married, the couple have two children, son Jesse and daughter Casse. The Whites live near Lake Washington, Seattle area. Jesse has worked as a ProTools engineer for Trevor Rabin.

**1981.** Chris Squire and Alan White attempt to fashion a band to be called XYZ, with Jimmy Page.

### Chris Squire:

*"That was fun, naturally. That came about because, unfortunately, it wasn't long after John Bonham had passed away, and Jimmy wanted to get back into playing, but he wanted to sort of ease into it. I can't remember exactly the first time I met Jimmy but in the '70s we were always at the same Melody Maker and New Musical Express awards lunches, so probably it was one of those. Plus Yes and Zeppelin were both Atlantic Records bands, so maybe I met him in the office. Anyway, because we lived relatively close to each other, in the Windsor area of England, we just ended up getting together and jamming. And Alan came in, and we just*

*played together and we were really just giving Jimmy some time to come back into enjoying playing again."*

*"Robert Plant was supposed to come and join us, but I think it was all a bit too early for him, after John Bonham had passed away. So he never actually made it to the studio. We just ended up doing four demos. But because Robert didn't want to come and go back to work at that point—and I understand why—the XYZ project never really became XYZ. It just got to the stage of becoming four demos. I was the singer but we didn't want to do a three-piece band."*

*"And actually parts of it have been used. We recorded the song 'Can You Imagine' on the Magnification album—that was one of the songs we had done with Jimmy. And there was another song that we did with him that went on the Firm album; I think they called it 'The Hunter' or something. Also, I'm not quite sure what album it was on—I'm going to say The Ladder— but there was a drum riff that Alan came up with. So bits of ideas from those sessions did end up getting recorded in various ways."*

### Alan White:

*"It was just a weird time when Chris and myself were floating free around London, and Steve was with Asia. We were released and people were doing different things. So Chris knew Jimmy Page pretty well, and he had a house on the river. Actually, a lot of the stuff that we did was written by Chris and myself. So we had ideas and we'd go down there and start work late in the afternoon and work into the early hours of the morning. It was quite an experimental period. It started to sound really good, and then management got involved and they had all these ideas which got in the way of the music, and that's kind of why it fell apart. I think Yes' manager wanted to be involved and then Peter Grant wanted to be involved, and they were at loggerheads on how to do this. They started to have a one-upmanship kind of thing."*

*"At one time Robert Plant came down and listened to the music, with a view to try to sing on some of it and see how he felt about it. But he just thought the music was too complicated, so it never panned out. But Jimmy was a lot of fun. On Led Zeppelin tracks, he used synthesizers with his guitar and things like that, so he's really into moving forward and being on the cutting edge of anything new. But he added the element of Zeppelin to it, so it was progressive rock meets Led Zeppelin."*

**January 1981.** Yes issue "Run to the Light"/"White Car" as a US single.

**February 12, 1981.** While Yes encounters difficulty due to their fragmented lineup, fellow proggers Rush attain their career peak with their classic eighth album *Moving Pictures*, issued this day. In contrast, over the ensuing years, as Rush stumbles with their attempts at modernization, Yes will find surprise success, as will both Asia and Genesis.

**July 1981.** Jon and Vangelis issue their sophomore album, *The Friends of Mr. Cairo* which scores a No.1 hit in Canada with the title track and goes platinum in that territory, for sales of over 100,000 copies. "State of Independence" would be covered at least three times, with Donna Summer scoring a hit with it in 1982. The album reaches No.64 on Billboard.

> *Billboard,* **on The Friends of Mr. Cairo:**
> *"Formerly of Yes, and Vangelis—who provided much of the music for the Cosmos soundtrack—are two of the leading forces in progressive music. In the past, these two have tended to take themselves too seriously but this effort is much lighter in tone and the better for it. The keyboard-dominated, classically-influenced music—overlayed with Anderson's chirping vocals—should find a home with Yes fans."*

**August 1, 1981.** The Buggles' "Video Killed the Radio Star" is the first video aired as MTV opens for business.

> **Geoff Downes:**
> *"It was something that was brought up after the event. Because at that time, we never really paid that much attention to it. MTV was just another cable channel. It was not readily available to all the homes in America. It was mainly the New York area, where I think it started originally. And then it quickly developed and we all started to think, this is going to be big, a lot bigger than we thought. So there was not a great deal of significance attached to that, because I think we felt, well, that's nice. It's nice to be the first video on that channel. But you know, it snowballed very, very quickly and developed into something much bigger."*

**September 22, 1981.** Robert Fripp re-constitutes and reinvigorates King Crimson with the landmark *Discipline* album. Two more would follow in the ersatz trilogy, *Beat* and *Three of a Perfect Pair*. Arguably, it is King Crimson—and at a similar heady creative level, Peter Gabriel—that brings excitement back to progressive rock, so that Genesis, Asia and Yes can clean up.

**October 1981.** With XYZ stalled, Chris Squire and Alan White issue a bright and cheery Christmas single on Atlantic called "Run with the Fox," orchestrated by Chris' long-time collaborator Andrew Jackman, with guest vocals by Chris' wife Nikki.

**November 11, 1981.** The Buggles issue their second and last album, *Adventures in Modern Recording*. The album includes a synth-pop version of Yes' "Into the Lens," re-titled "I Am a Camera." Two demo tracks from the album's sessions would be reworked for Yes' 2011 studio album, *Fly from Here*.

> **Geoff Downes:**
> *"We had our spell with Yes, and then we went back and made the second Buggles album. The difference between those albums bears, really, a lot of influence with Yes in the middle of it—that's how best I can describe that."*

**November 30, 1981.** Yes issue a hits pack called *Classic Yes*, which eventually sells platinum. The original vinyl issue includes a 7" that plays at 33 1/3 rpm and features live renditions of "Roundabout" and "I've Seen All Good People." *Classic Yes* is in essence the most widely recognised

Yes compilation. The album—with its very pretty cover art—marks the end of an era, with Yes soon to write history as the biggest progressive rock comeback story the genre had ever seen.

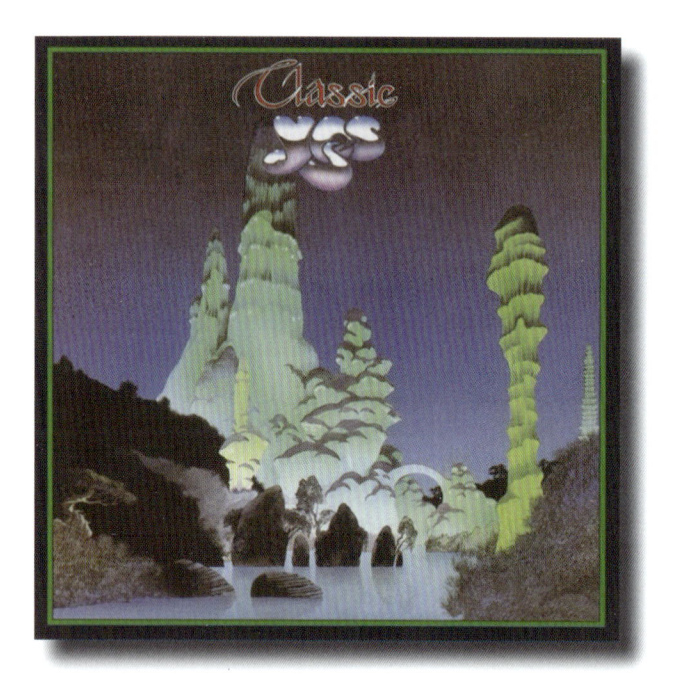

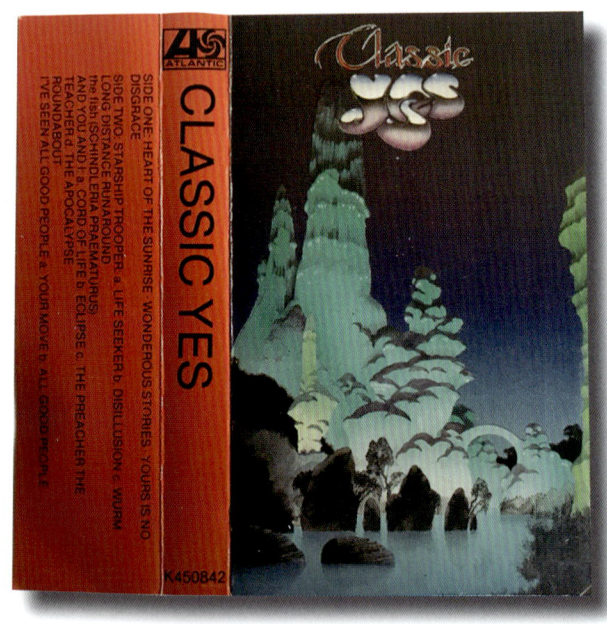

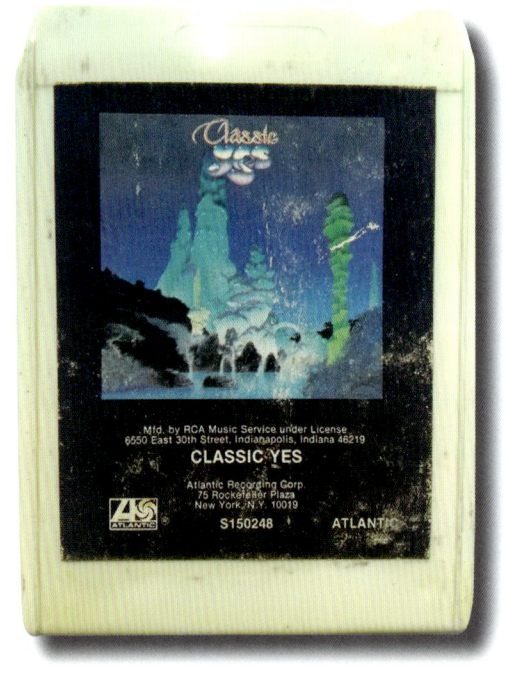

**Rick Wakeman:**
*"I'm a great 90125 fan. I think 90125 is one of the most important albums Yes has ever created. Because I think without 90125, there wouldn't be a Yes now. Because it was that period in the '80s, the mid '80s, where prog rock was dead—really dead—and bands like Yes were in a death throe. A lot of bands were. So the album... I know it was originally a different name, and then Jon came in and sang on it and various things, and then it became a Yes album. But because it was so, shall we say un-Yes in various respects, but with Jon's classic voice stuck over the top, it just about fit into a genre that was acceptable without it being prog rock, if you know what I mean. Very song-oriented, great Trevor Horn production. I mean, I'm a great Trevor Horn fan, and of course, not so much in the UK and in Europe, but certainly in America, it was a monster album, and I'm convinced that saved the life of the band. I'm convinced if the band did another album like Drama or something like that, the band wouldn't be here now. It wouldn't have survived."*

# Selected Discography

A few points of methodology are in order. By necessity toward compactness, I've prioritized along the following lines. Most important, in my opinion are the studio albums in their original form and the songs upon them (no double quote marks, for neatness). I thought timings were of interest as well, given the band's often radically long songs.

I've used a note section as a catch-all for anything else I thought important, i.e. mostly lineup changes. For personnel, I've simplified and credited the performers with their main role or duty only, establishing the full lineup for the debut and then just noting alterations as we move from album to album.

As well, I've given these albums a side 1/side 2 designation, given that we are dealing exclusively with the vinyl era with this timeline.

## 1. Studio Albums

*Yes*
July 1969; produced by Paul Clay and Yes
Side 1: 1. Beyond and Before (4:50) 2. I See You (6:33) 3. Yesterday and Today (2:37) 4. Looking Around (3:49)
Side 2: 1. Harold Land (5:26) 2. Every Little Thing (5:24) 3. Sweetness (4:19) 4. Survival (6:01)
Notes: Jon Anderson – lead vocals; Peter Banks – guitar; Tony Kaye – organ, piano; Chris Squire – bass; Bill Bruford – drums.

*Time and a Word*
July 1970; produced by Tony Colton
Side 1: 1. No Opportunity Necessary, No Experience Needed 2. Then (5:42) 3. Everydays (6:06) 4. Sweet Dreams (3:48)
Side 2: 1. The Prophet (6:32) 2. Clear Days (2:04) 3. Astral Traveller (5:50) 4. Time and a Word (4:31)

*The Yes Album*
February 1971; produced by Yes and Eddie Offord
Side 1: 1. Yours is No Disgrace (9:36) 2.The Clap (3:07) 3. Starship Trooper a. Life Seeker b. Dissolution c. Würm (9:23)
Side 2: 1. I've Seen All Good People a. Your Move b. All Good People (6:47) 2. A Venture (3.13) 4. Perpetual Change (8:50)
Notes: Guitarist Steve Howe replaces Peter Banks.

*Fragile*
November 1971; produced by Yes and Eddie Offord
Side 1: 1. Roundabout (8:30) 2. Cans and Brahms (1:38) 3. We Have Heaven(1:40) 4. South Side of the Sky (8:02)
Side 2 1. Five Per Cent For Nothing (0:35) 2. Long Distance Runaround (3:30) 3. The Fish (Schindleria Praematurus) (2:39) 4. Mood for a Day (3:00). 5. Heart of the Sunrise (11:27)
Notes: Keyboardist Rick Wakeman replaces Tony Kaye.

*Close to the Edge*
September 1972; produced by Yes and Eddie Offord
Side 1: 1. Close to the Edge I. The Solid Time of Change II. Total Mass Retain III. I Get Up I Get Down IV. Seasons of Man (18:50)
Side 2: 1. And You and I I. Cord of Life II. Eclipse III. The Preacher the Teacher IV. Apocalypse (10:09) 2. Siberian Khatru (8:57)

*Tales from Topographic Oceans*
December 1973; produced by Yes and Eddie Offord
Side 1: The Revealing Science of God (Dance of the Dawn) (20:27)
Side 2: The Remembering (High the Memory) (20:38)
Side 3: The Ancient (Giants Under the Sun) (18:34)
Side 4: Ritual (Nous Sommes du Soleil) (21:35)
Notes: Drummer Alan White replaces Bill Bruford.

*Relayer*
November 1974; produced by Yes and Eddie Offord
Side 1: The Gates of Delirium (21:55)
Side 2: 1. Sound Chaser (9:25) 2. To Be Over (9:08)
Notes: Keyboardist Patrick Moraz replaces Rick Wakeman.

218

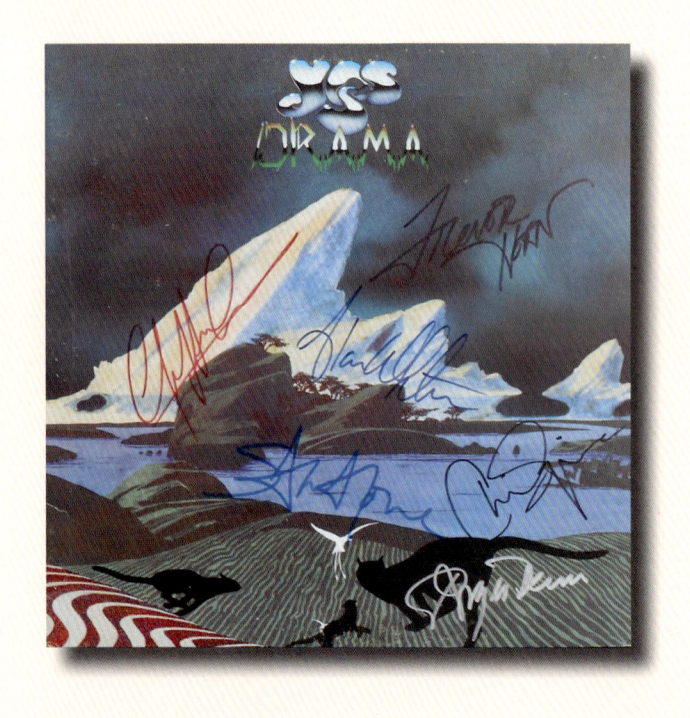

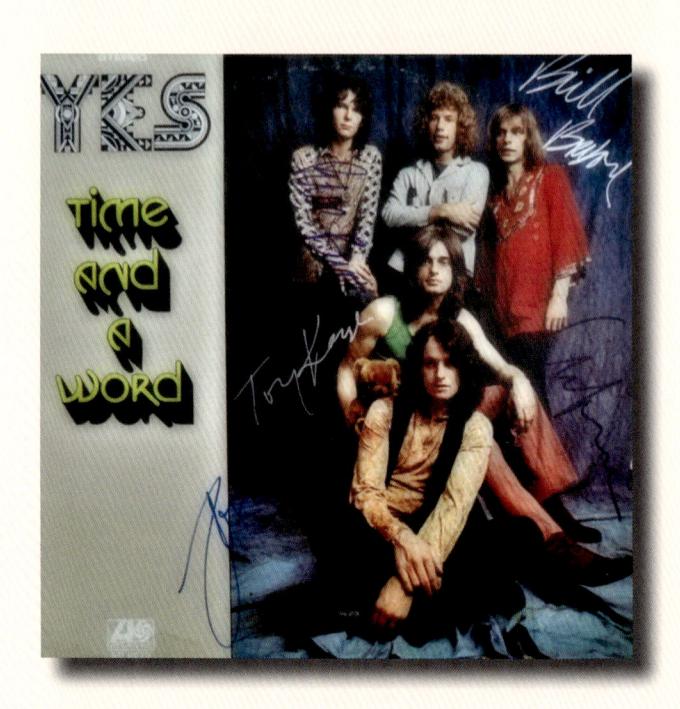

*Going for the One*
July 1977; produced by Yes
Side 1: 1. Going for the One (5:30) 2. Turn of the Century (7:58) 3. Parallels (5:52)
Side 2: 1. Wonderous Stories (3:45) 2. Awaken (15:38)
Notes: Returning keyboardist Rick Wakeman replaces Patrick Moraz.

*Tormato*
September 1978; produced by Yes
Side 1: 1. a. Future Times b. Rejoice (6:46) 2. Don't Kill the Whale (3:55) 3. Madrigal (2:21) 4. Release, Release (5:40)
Side 2: 1. Arriving UFO (6:02) 2. Circus of Heaven (4:28) 3. Onward (4:00) 4. On the Silent Wings of Freedom (7:45)

*Drama*
August 1980; produced by Yes
Side 1: 1. Machine Messiah (10:27) 2. White Car (1:21) 3. Does It Really Happen? (6:34)
Side 2: 1. Into the Lens (8:31) 2. Run Through the Light (4:39) 3. Tempus Fugit (5:14)
Notes: Keyboardist Geoff Downes replaces Rick Wakeman; vocalist Trevor Horn replaces Jon Anderson.

## 2. Live albums

*Yessongs*
May 1973; produced by Yes and Eddie Offord
Side 1: 1. Opening (Excerpt from "Firebird Suite") (3:45) 2. Siberian Khatru (8:50) 3. Heart of the Sunrise (11:26)
Side 2: 1. Perpetual Change (14:08) 2. And You and I (9:55)
Side 3: 1. Mood for a Day (2:52) 2. Excerpts from "The Six Wives of Henry VIII" (6:35) 3. Roundabout (8:33)
Side 4: 1. I've Seen All Good People (7:00) 2. Long Distance Runaround (13:45)
Side 5: 1. Close to the Edge (18:41)
Side 6: 1. Yours Is No Disgrace (14:21) 2. Starship Trooper (9:25)

*Yesshows*
November 1980; produced by Chris Squire
Side 1: 1. Parallels (6:57) 2. Time and a Word (4:05) 3. Going for the One (5:13)
Side 2: 1. The Gates of Delirium (22:58)
Side 3: 1. Don't Kill the Whale (4:12) 2. Ritual (Part 1) (12:13)
Side 4: 1. Ritual (Part 2) (16:09) 2. Wonderous Stories (3:55)

## 3. Selected compilations

*Yesterdays*
February 1975; various producers
Side 1: 1. America (10:31) 2. Looking Around (3:59) 3. Time and a Word (4:31) 4. Sweet Dreams (3:47)
Side 2: 1. Then (5:46) 2. Survival (6:20) 3. Astral Traveller (5:53) 4. Dear Father (4:18)
Notes: Selections from *Yes* and *Time and a Word* plus the band's cover of Paul Simon's "America" plus a non-LP B-side called "Dear Father."

*Classic Yes*
November 1981; produced by Yes and Eddie Offord
Side 1: 1. Heart of the Sunrose (10:32) 2. Wonderous Stories (3:45) 3. Yours Is No Disgrace (9:41)
Side 2: 1. Starship Trooper (9:26) 2. Long Distance Runaround (3:33) 3. The Fish (2:35) 4. And You and I (10:07)

# Interviews by the Author

Anderson, Jon. May 14, 2015.
Bachman, Randy. October 28, 2002.
Bruford, Bill. April 15, 2002.
Downes, Geoff. September 27, 2002.
Downes, Geoff. April 11, 2013.
Howe, Steve. September 3, 2001.
Howe, Steve. November 16, 2002.
Sherwood, Billy. May 6, 2015.
Squire, Chris. August 6, 2011.
Squire, Chris. March 28, 2014.
Wakeman, Rick. May 7, 2004.
Ward, Bill. May 1, 2015.
White, Alan. August 6, 2011.
White, Alan. June 16, 2014.

Rick Wakeman

YESSONGS

Yes Solos
LP SAMPLER

The Yes Album

Tales From
Topographic Oceans
YES

Looking Around
ATLANTIC
ATL 70425
45-RPM-SINGLE
YES
Every
Little
Thing

# Additional Citations

Banks, Peter, with Billy James. Beyond and Before: The Formative Years of Yes. Golden Treasures Publishing Ltd., Bentonville, Arkansas. 2001.
Billboard. *Olias of Sunhillow* record review. July 10, 1976.
Billboard. *Drama* record review. August 30, 1980.
Billboard. *The Friends of Mr. Cairo* record review. July 25, 1981.
Cash Box. *Relayer* record review. December 21, 1974.
Cash Box. Yes. September 17, 1977.
Cash Box. Ertegun Relates His Views on Yes International Appeal by Ahmet Ertegun. September 17, 1977.
Circus. Squire and Howe Sire Solo Yessongs by Leo Warner. No. 108. April 1975.
Circus. Yestour '76 by Peter Crescenti. No. 139. September 13, 1976.
Circus. Yes is Going for the Big One by Jim Farber. No. 163. September 8, 1977.
Classic Rock. Yes: Rock's True Pioneers by Sal Treppiedi. Spring 1988.
Classic Rock Revisited. Interview with Steve Howe by Roy Rahl. September 8, 2014.
Crawdaddy. Henry VIII's Yes Man by Jon Swenson. August 1973.
Creem. *Tormato* record review by Michael Davis. Vol. 10, No. 8. January 1979.
Creem. *Drama* record review by Rick Johnson. Vol. 12, No. 7. December 1980.
Gettin' Off. Rick Wakeman: Journey to the centre. Reprinted from New World Magazine. Consumer Edition No.1. 1973.
Goldmine. Yes Through the Years by Howard Whitman. Issue 796. Volume 37, No. 2. February 2011.
Hit Parader. The New Yes: The Drama Continues by Dan Hedges. No. 198. January 1981.
Keyboard. What Ever Happened To Patrick Moraz? by Robert L. Doerschuk. May 1991.
Keyboard. Bruford & White: Beating Off With High-Tech Toys by Greg Rule. Vol. 17, No. 8., Issue No. 184. August 1991.
Keyboard. Rick Wakeman & Tony Kaye Face Off by Robert L. Doerschuk. Vol. 17, No. 8., Issue No. 184. August 1991.
Melody Maker. YES - now with added Whiteness by Chris Charlesworth. July 29, 1972.
Melody Maker. *Tales from Topographic Oceans* record review by Chris Welch. December 1, 1973.
Melody Maker. Yes – Over the Edge by Chris Welch. December 1, 1973.
Melody Maker. Greek Coup... by Steve Lake. August 10, 1974.
Melody Maker. Cover story by Karl Dallas. August 17, 1974.
Melody Maker. Wondrous Stories by Chris Welch. October 22, 1977.
Music Express. This combo Buggles the imagination by David Farrell. Vol. 4, No. 10. 1980.
New Musical Express. *Tales from Topographic Oceans* record review by Steve Clarke. January 19, 1974.
New Musical Express. Wakeman - on Wembley ice! April 5, 1975.
Phonograph. *Relayer* record review by Ed Sciaky. Vol. 5, No. 4. January 1975.
Record Collector. Yes on Yes. No. 269. January 2002.
Record Collector. Yesteryears by Tim Jones. No. 269. January 2002.
Record Mirror. *Time and a Word* record review by R.P. July 25, 1970.
Record Mirror. James Craig in Los Angeles on Tour with Yes. April 21, 1973.
Record Mirror. Yes – What a Fine Climax to Reach by Roy Hill. February 2, 1974.
Record Mirror. Cosmic Nonsense? by Robin Smith. October 29, 1977.
Rolling Stone. *Going for the One* record review by John Swenson. September 8, 1977.
Sea of Tranquility. An Interview with the Legendary Jon Anderson by Jordan Blum. May 1, 2011.
Something Else Reviews. 'It was a perfect storm:' Trevor Rabin and Jon Anderson on Yes' most overlooked album by Nick Deriso. May 10, 2014.
Trouser Press. Wakeman Tells Yesstories by Ira Robbins. No. 20. June/July 1977.
Trouser Press. Bill Bruford conjures up his past by Ray Bonici. No. 31. August 1978.
Universal Wheels. Alan White Talks! by Kevin Julie. 2000.
Universal Wheels. Interview with Geoff Downes by Kevin Julie. 2012.

# Special Thanks

Besides my own interviews and material cited in Additional Sources, two buddies—Dmitry Epstein and Jeb Wright—have graciously allowed me to quote from some of their chats.

Dmitry's smart and historical classic rock scholarship can be seen at dmme.net. So proud of him coming to Toronto, pretty much cold, from Belarus via Israel and carving a good life for him and his family very, very quickly.

Jeb... what can I say about Jeb? Through his fine work at classicrockrevisted.com (now retired), he's proven himself to be the most important supporter of classic rock we've got. Without his words of wisdom and grounded perspective on all these guys we talk to when we get on an email tear or on one of our epic phone calls, I doubt I'd be able to keep plowing ahead. Friggin' inspiration, that guy. Look for his fiction—yes, fiction—soon.

Finally a speacial thanks to Doug Curran and Keith Hoisington, who kindly supplied tour photos and memorabilia, plus Agustin Garcia de Paredes with his studious proof-reading of this new edition.

# Martin Popoff – A Complete Bibliography

2021: Loud 'n' Proud: Fifty Years of Nazareth, Driven: Rush in the '90s and "In the End," Uriah Heep: A Visual Biography, Flaming Telepaths: Imaginos Expanded and Specified, Rebel Rouser: A Sweet User Manual

2020: The Fortune: On the Rocks with Angel, Van Halen: A Visual Biography, Limelight: Rush in the '80s, Thin Lizzy: A Visual Biography, Empire of the Clouds: Iron Maiden in the 2000s, Blue Öyster Cult: A Visual Biography, Anthem: Rush in the '70s, Denim and Leather: Saxon's First Ten Years, Black Funeral: Into the Coven with Mercyful Fate

2019: Satisfaction: 10 Albums That Changed My Life, Holy Smoke: Iron Maiden in the '90s, Sensitive to Light: The Rainbow Story, Where Eagles Dare: Iron Maiden in the '80s, Aces High: The Top 250 Heavy Metal Songs of the '80s, Judas Priest: Turbo 'til Now, Born Again! Black Sabbath in the Eighties and Nineties

2018: Riff Raff: The Top 250 Heavy Metal Songs of the '70s, Lettin' Go: UFO in the '80s and '90s, Queen: Album by Album, Unchained: A Van Halen User Manual, Iron Maiden: Album by Album, Sabotage! Black Sabbath in the Seventies, Welcome to My Nightmare: 50 Years of Alice Cooper, Judas Priest: Decade of Domination, Popoff Archive – 6: American Power Metal, Popoff Archive – 5: European Power Metal, The Clash: All the Albums, All the Songs

2017: Led Zeppelin: All the Albums, All the Songs, AC/DC: Album by Album, Lights Out: Surviving the '70s with UFO, Tornado of Souls: Thrash's Titanic Clash, Caught in a Mosh: The Golden Era of Thrash, Rush: Album by Album, Beer Drinkers and Hell Raisers: The Rise of Motörhead, Metal Collector: Gathered Tales from Headbangers, Hit the Lights: The Birth of Thrash, Popoff Archive – 4: Classic Rock, Popoff Archive – 3: Hair Metal

2016: Popoff Archive – 2: Progressive Rock, Popoff Archive – 1: Doom Metal, Rock the Nation: Montrose, Gamma and Ronnie Redefined, Punk Tees: The Punk Revolution in 125 T-Shirts, Metal Heart: Aiming High with Accept, Ramones at 40, Time and a Word: The Yes Story

2015: Kickstart My Heart: A Mötley Crüe Day-by-Day, This Means War: The Sunset Years of the NWOBHM, Wheels of Steel: The Explosive Early Years of the NWOBHM, Swords and Tequila: Riot's Classic First Decade, Who Invented Heavy Metal?, Sail Away: Whitesnake's Fantastic Voyage

2014: Live Magnetic Air: The Unlikely Saga of the Superlative Max Webster, Steal Away the Night: An Ozzy Osbourne Day-by-Day, The Big Book of Hair Metal, Sweating Bullets: The Deth and Rebirth of Megadeth, Smokin' Valves: A Headbanger's Guide to 900 NWOBHM Records

2013: The Art of Metal (co-edit with Malcolm Dome), 2 Minutes to Midnight: An Iron Maiden Day-by-Day, Metallica: The Complete Illustrated History, Rush: The Illustrated History, Ye Olde Metal: 1979, Scorpions: Top of the Bill - updated and reissued as Wind of Change: The Scorpions Story in 2016

2012: Epic Ted Nugent, Fade To Black: Hard Rock Cover Art of the Vinyl Age, It's Getting Dangerous: Thin Lizzy 81-12, We Will Be Strong: Thin Lizzy 76-81, Fighting My Way Back: Thin Lizzy 69-76, The Deep Purple Royal Family: Chain of Events '80 – '11, The Deep Purple Royal Family: Chain of Events Through '79 - reissued as The Deep Purple Family Year by Year books

2011: Black Sabbath FAQ, The Collector's Guide to Heavy Metal: Volume 4: The '00s (co-authored with David Perri)

2010: Goldmine Standard Catalog of American Records 1948 – 1991, 7th Edition

2009: Goldmine Record Album Price Guide, 6th Edition, Goldmine 45 RPM Price Guide, 7th Edition, A Castle Full of Rascals: Deep Purple '83 – '09, Worlds Away: Voivod and the Art of Michel Langevin, Ye Olde Metal: 1978

2008: Gettin' Tighter: Deep Purple '68 – '76, All Access: The Art of the Backstage Pass, Ye Olde Metal: 1977, Ye Olde Metal: 1976

2007: Judas Priest: Heavy Metal Painkillers, Ye Olde Metal: 1973 to 1975, The Collector's Guide to Heavy Metal: Volume 3: The Nineties, Ye Olde Metal: 1968 to 1972

2006: Run for Cover: The Art of Derek Riggs, Black Sabbath: Doom Let Loose, Dio: Light Beyond the Black

2005: The Collector's Guide to Heavy Metal: Volume 2: The Eighties, Rainbow: English Castle Magic, UFO: Shoot Out the Lights, The New Wave of British Heavy Metal Singles

2004: Blue Öyster Cult: Secrets Revealed! – update and reissue 2009); updated and reissued as Agents of Fortune: The Blue Öyster Cult Story 2016, Contents Under Pressure: 30 Years of Rush at Home & Away, The Top 500 Heavy Metal Albums of All Time

2003: The Collector's Guide to Heavy Metal: Volume 1: The Seventies, The Top 500 Heavy Metal Songs of All Time

2001: Southern Rock Review

2000: Heavy Metal: 20th Century Rock and Roll, The Goldmine Price Guide to Heavy Metal Records

1997: The Collector's Guide to Heavy Metal

1993: Riff Kills Man! 25 Years of Recorded Hard Rock & Heavy Metal

*See martinpopoff.com for complete details and ordering information.*

© Alan Perry

# About the Author

At approximately 7900 (with over 7000 appearing in his books), Martin has unofficially written more record reviews than anybody in the history of music writing across all genres. Additionally, Martin has penned approximately 90 books on hard rock, heavy metal, classic rock and record collecting. He was Editor-In-Chief of the now retired Brave Words & Bloody Knuckles, Canada's foremost metal publication for 14 years, and has also contributed to Revolver, Guitar World, Goldmine, Record Collector, bravewords.com, lollipop.com and hardradio.com, with many record label band bios and liner notes to his credit as well. Additionally, Martin has been a regular contractor to Banger Films, having worked for two years as researcher on the award-winning documentary *Rush: Beyond the Lighted Stage*, on the writing and research team for the 11-episode Metal Evolution and on the ten-episode Rock Icons, both for VH1 Classic. Additionally, Martin is the writer of the original metal genre chart used in *Metal: A Headbanger's Journey* and throughout the Metal Evolution episodes. Martin currently resides in Toronto and can be reached through martinp@inforamp.net or www.martinpopoff.com.

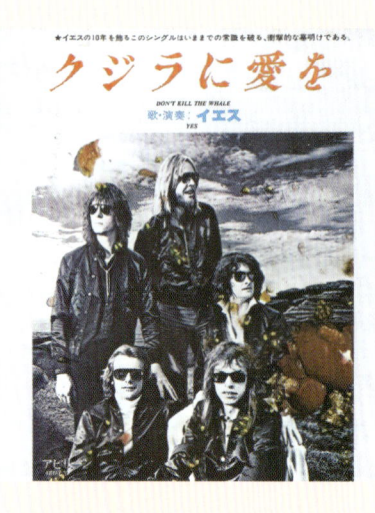

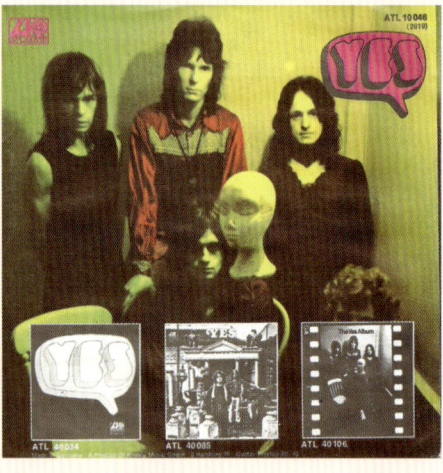

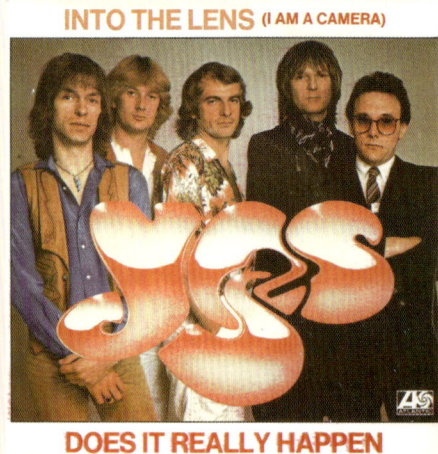

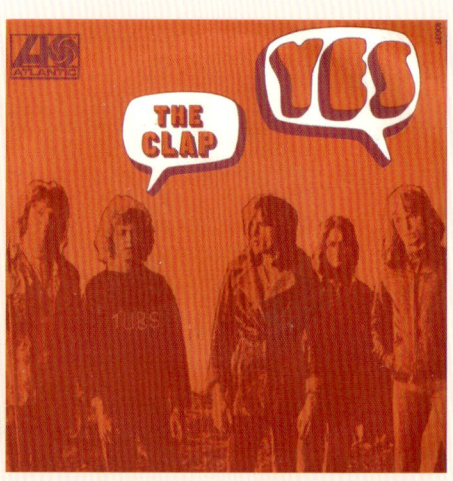

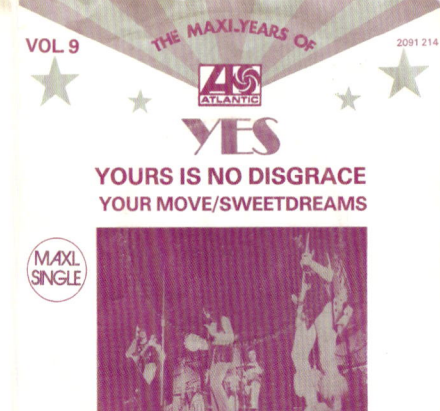

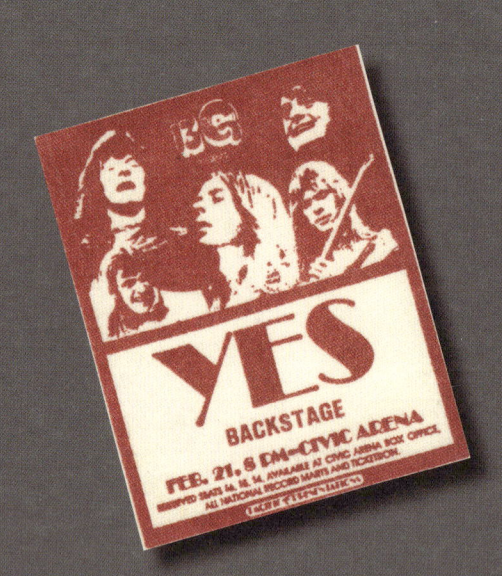

1976 U.S. TOUR STAGE PASS

YES BACKSTAGE
FEB. 21, 6 PM—CIVIC ARENA

YES TORMATO
WEMBLEY ARENA
28th Oct. 1978
Non Restricted
GUEST PASS